Lucky Pants
and Other Golf Myths

Also by Joe Kohl

Marital Bliss and Other Oxymorons

Unspeakably Rotten Cartoons

LuCKy PANtS

and Other Golf Myths

Joe Kohl
Introduction by Dave Barry

Mustang Publishing
Memphis, TN • USA

Published in the United States of America by Mustang Publishing Company, Inc., P.O. Box 3004, Memphis, TN 38173. Manufactured and printed in the USA.

Library of Congress Cataloging-in-Publication Data

Kohl, Joe.
Lucky pants and other golf myths / Joe Kohl ; introduction by Dave Barry.
p. cm.
ISBN 0-914457-80-2 (alk. paper)
1. Golf–Caricatures and cartoons. 2. American wit and humor, Pictorial.
I. Title.
NC1429.K59A4 1996
741.5'973–dc20 96-20826
CIP

Printed on acid-free paper.

10 9 8 7 6 5 4 3 2 1

To my wife Phyllis,
with love

Acknowledgments

I would like to offer my sincere thanks to Dr. Harold Isaacson and Walt Kopy for their help and inspiration.

Also, I'd like to dedicate this book to the memory of Stan Cohen, whose encouragement made this all possible.

Joe Kohl

Introduction

Dave Barry

Nobody knows exactly how golf got started. Probably what happened was, thousands of years ago, a couple of primitive guys were standing around, holding some odd-shaped sticks, and they noticed a golf ball lying on the grass, and they said, "Hey! Let's see if we can hit this into a hole!" And then they said, "Nah, let's just tell long, boring anecdotes about it instead."

Which is basically the object, in golf. You put on the most unattractive pants that money can buy, pants so ugly that they have to be manufactured by blind people in dark rooms, and you get together in the clubhouse with other golfers and drone away for hours about how you "bogeyed" your three-iron on the par six, or your six-iron on the par three, or whatever. Also, you watch endless televised professional golf tournaments with names like the Buick Merrill Lynch Manufacturers Hanover Frito-Lay Ti-D-Bol

88

Preparation H Classic, which consist entirely of moderately overweight men holding clubs and frowning into the distance while, in the background, two announcers hold interminable whispered conversations like this:

FIRST ANNOUNCER: Bob, he's lying about eighteen yards from the green with a fourteen-mile-per-hour wind out of the northeast, a relative humidity of seventy two percent, and a chance of afternoon or evening thundershowers. He might use a nine-iron here.

SECOND ANNOUNCER: Or possibly an eight, Bill. Or even—this makes me so excited that I almost want to speak in a normal tone of voice—a seven.

FIRST ANNOUNCER: Or he could just keep on frowning into space. Remember that one time we had a profes sional golfer frown for five solid hours, never once hitting a ball, us whispering the whole time in between Buick commercials, and it turned out he'd had some kind of seizure and died, standing up, grip ping his sand wedge?

SECOND ANNOUNCER: In that situation, Bill, I'd have used a putter.

If you *really* get into golf, you can actually try to play it some time, although this is not a requirement. I did it once, with a friend of mine named Paul, who is an avid golfer in the sense that if he had to choose between playing golf and ensuring permanent world peace, he'd want to know how many holes.

So we got out on the golf course in one of those little electric carts that golfers ride around in to avoid the danger that they might actually have to contract some muscle tissue. Also, we had an enormous collection of random clubs and at least 3,000 balls, which turned out to be not nearly enough.

The way we played was, first Paul would hit his ball directly toward the hole. This is basic golfing strategy: You want to hit the ball the least possible number of times so you can get back to the clubhouse to tell boring anecdotes and drink. When it was my turn, we'd drive the cart to wherever my ball was, which sometimes meant taking the interstate highway. When we finally arrived at our destination, Paul would examine the situation and suggest a club.

"Try a five-iron here," he'd say, as if he honestly believed it would make a difference.

Then, with a straight face, he'd give me very specific directions as to where I should hit the ball. "You want to aim it about two and a half yards to the right of that fourth palm tree," he'd say, pointing at a palm tree that I could not hit with a Strategic Defense Initiative laser. I'd frown, pro-golfer-style, at this tree, then I'd haul off and take a violent swing at the ball, taking care to keep my head down, which is an important part of your golf stroke because it gives you a legal excuse if the ball winds up lodged in somebody's brain.

Sometimes, after my swing, the ball would still be there, surrounded by a miniature scene of devastation, similar to the view that airborne politicians have of federal disaster areas. Sometimes the ball would be gone, which was the signal to look up and see how hard Paul was trying not to laugh. Usually he was trying very hard, which meant the ball had gone about as far as you would hide an Easter egg from a small child with impaired vision. But sometimes the ball had completely disappeared, and we'd look for it, but we'd never see it again. I think it went into another dimension, a parallel universe where people are still talking about the strange day when these golf balls started materializing out of thin air, right in the middle of dinner parties, concerts, etc.

So anyway, by following this golfing procedure, Paul and I were able to complete nine entire holes in less time than it would have taken us to memorize *Moby Dick* in Korean. We agreed that nine holes was plenty for a person with my particular level of liability insurance, so we headed back to the clubhouse for a beer, which, despite being a novice at golf, I was able to swallow with absolutely no trouble. The trick is to keep your head up.

"Golf does strange things to people.
It makes liars out of honest men,
cheats out of altruists,
cowards out of brave men,
and fools out of everybody."
Milton Gross

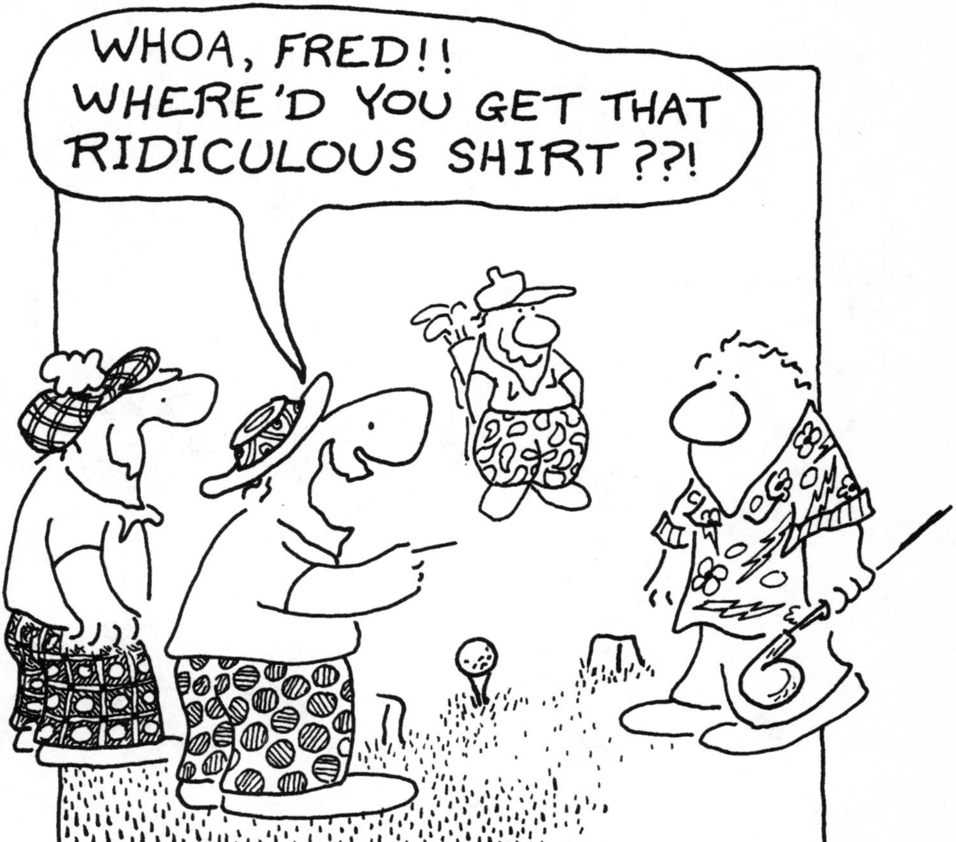
WHOA, FRED!! WHERE'D YOU GET THAT RIDICULOUS SHIRT??!

GOLF MYTH #307

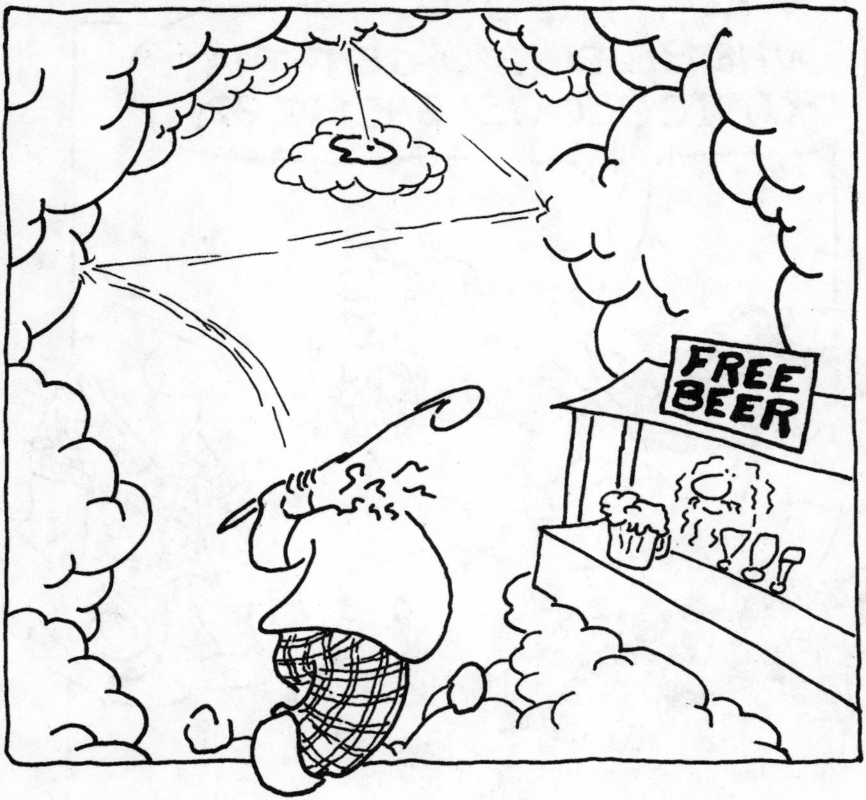
FREE
BEER

GOLF HEAVEN

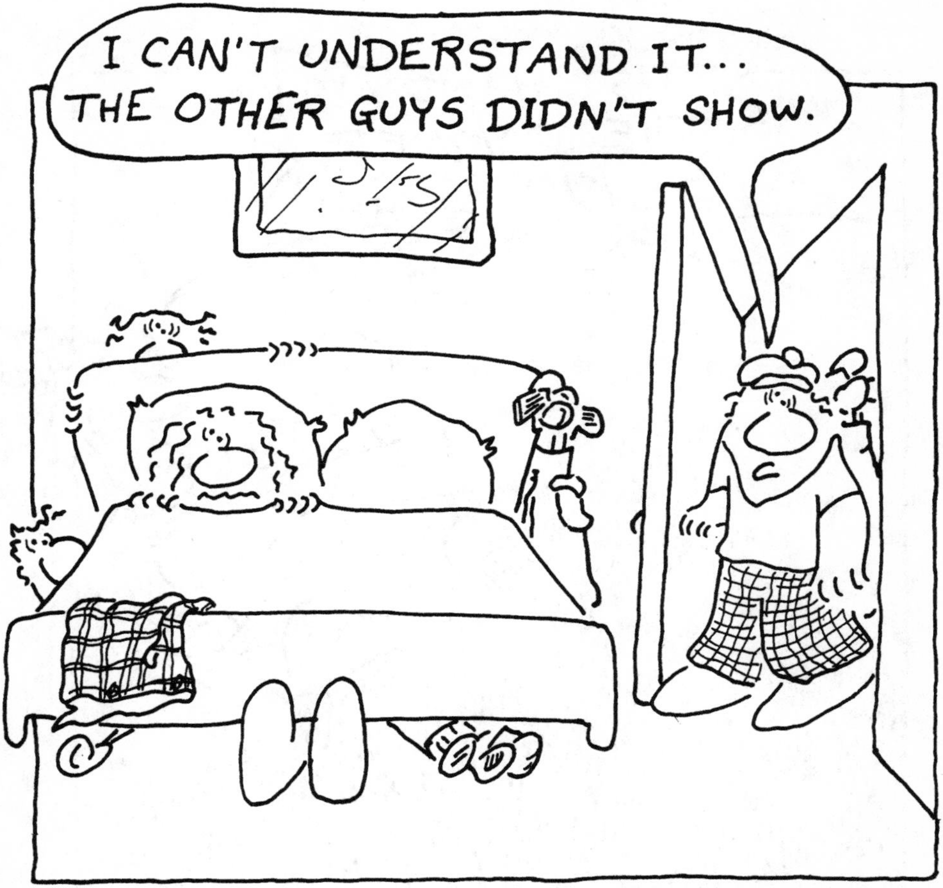
I CAN'T UNDERSTAND IT...
THE OTHER GUYS DIDN'T SHOW.

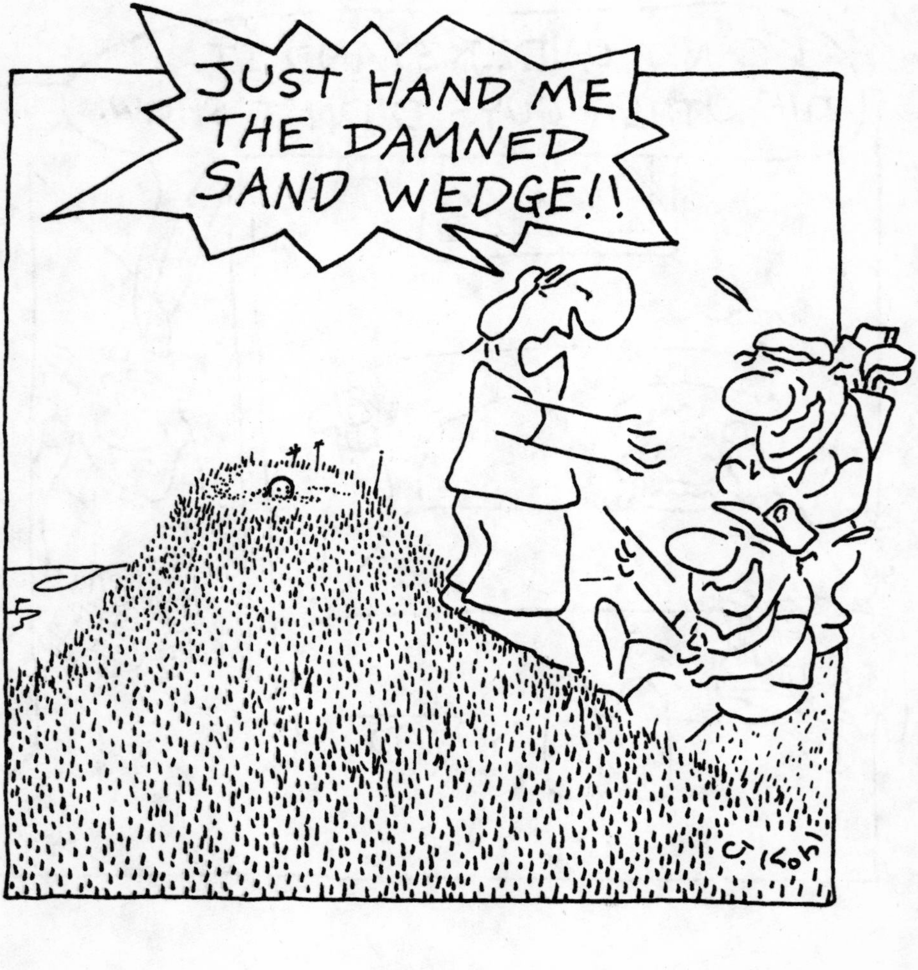
JUST HAND ME THE DAMNED SAND WEDGE!!
C. Koh

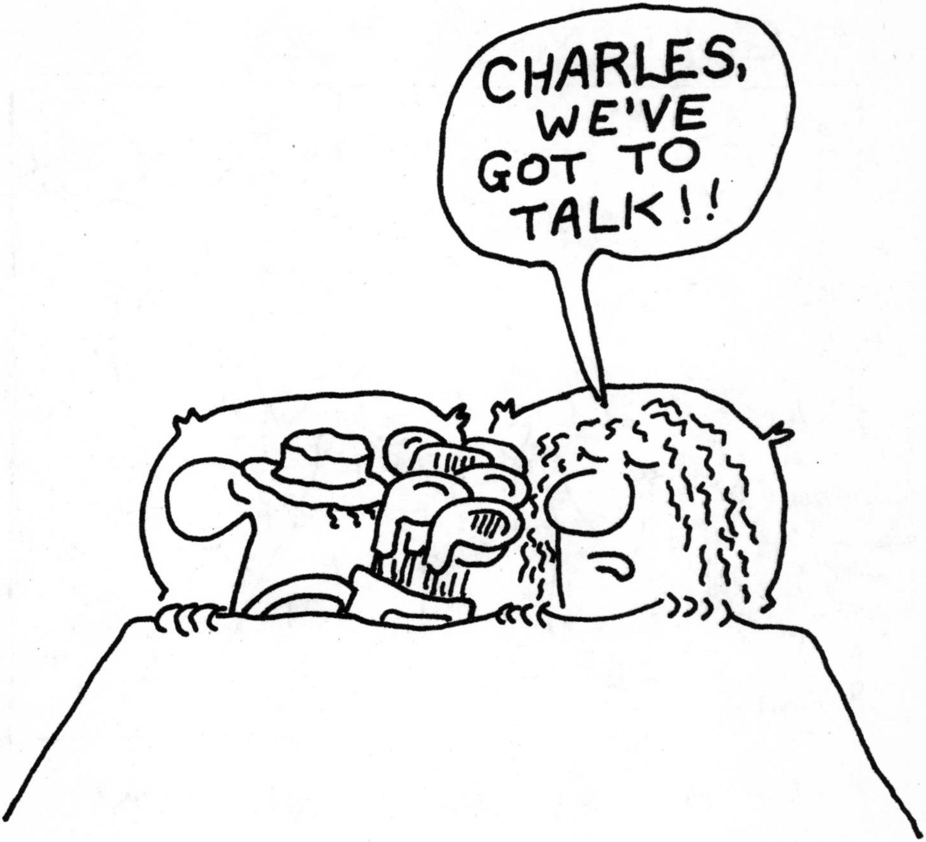
CHARLES, WE'VE GOT TO TALK!!

GOLF MYTH #293

THE BALL WASHER NOBODY MAKES OBSCENE JOKES ABOUT

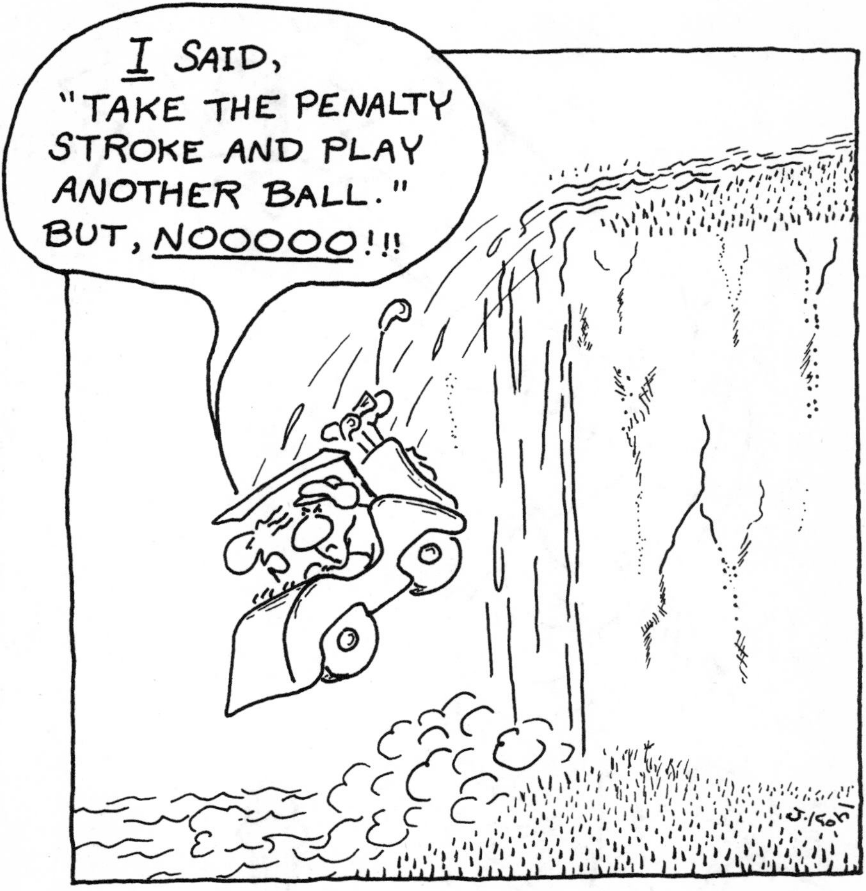
I SAID, "TAKE THE PENALTY STROKE AND PLAY ANOTHER BALL." BUT, NOOOOO!!!
J. Kohl

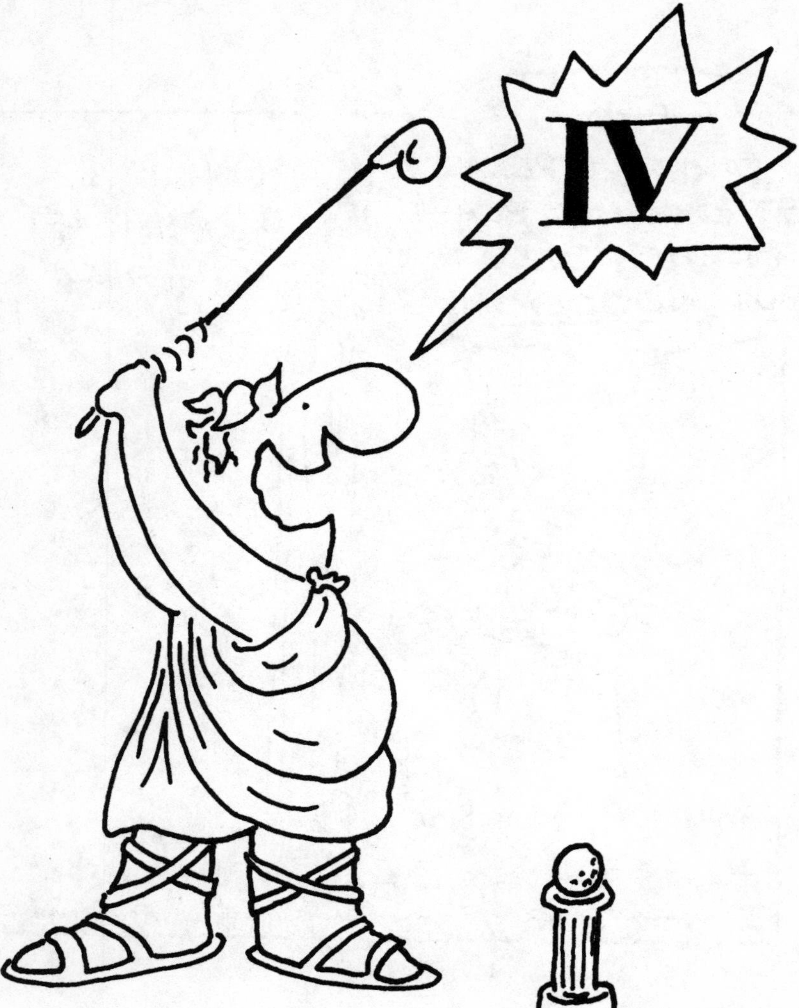
IV

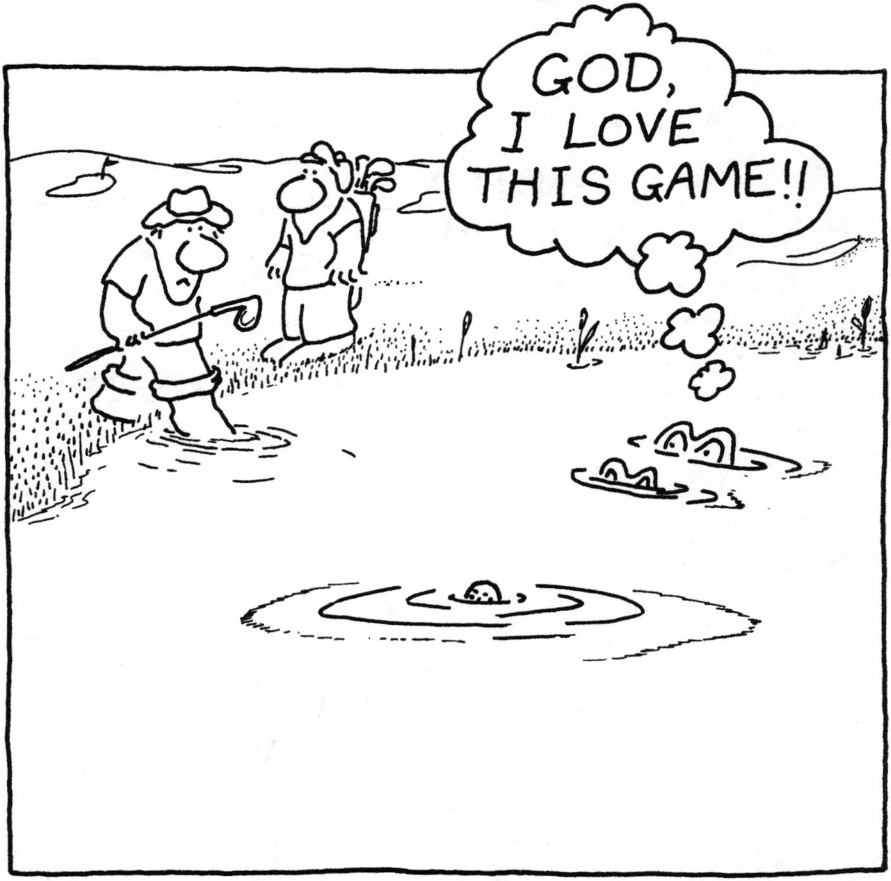
GOD, I LOVE THIS GAME!!

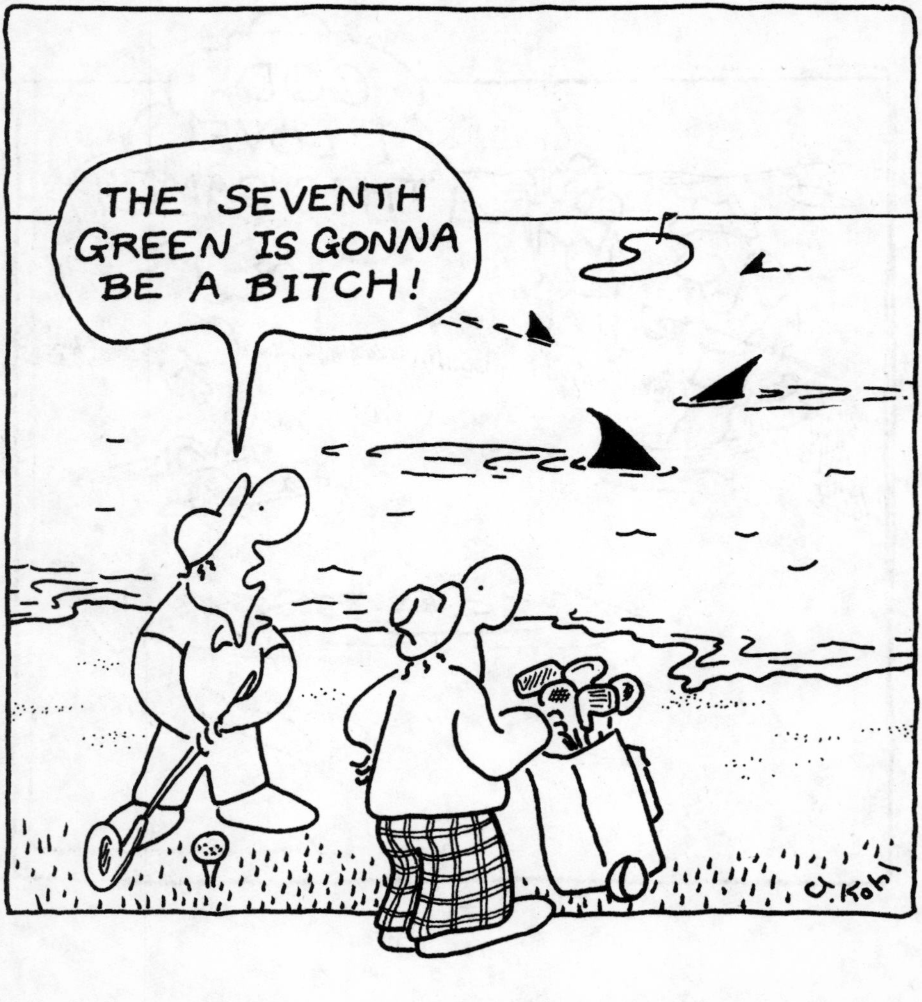
THE SEVENTH GREEN IS GONNA BE A BITCH!
J. Kohl

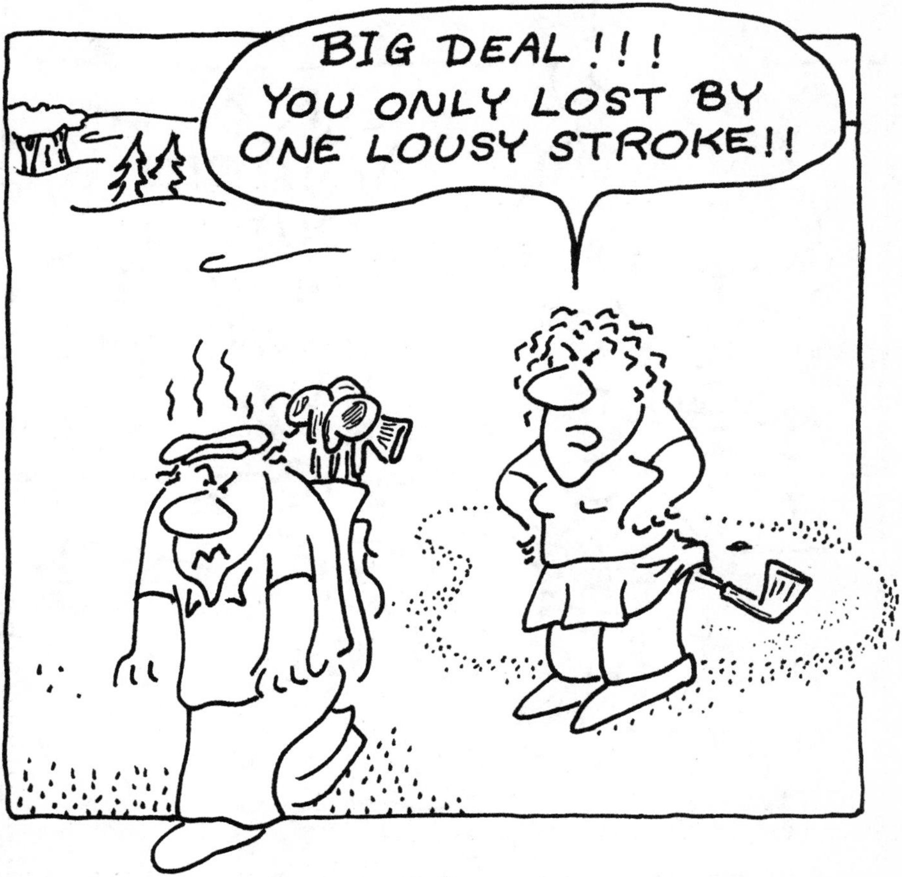
BIG DEAL !!! YOU ONLY LOST BY ONE LOUSY STROKE!!

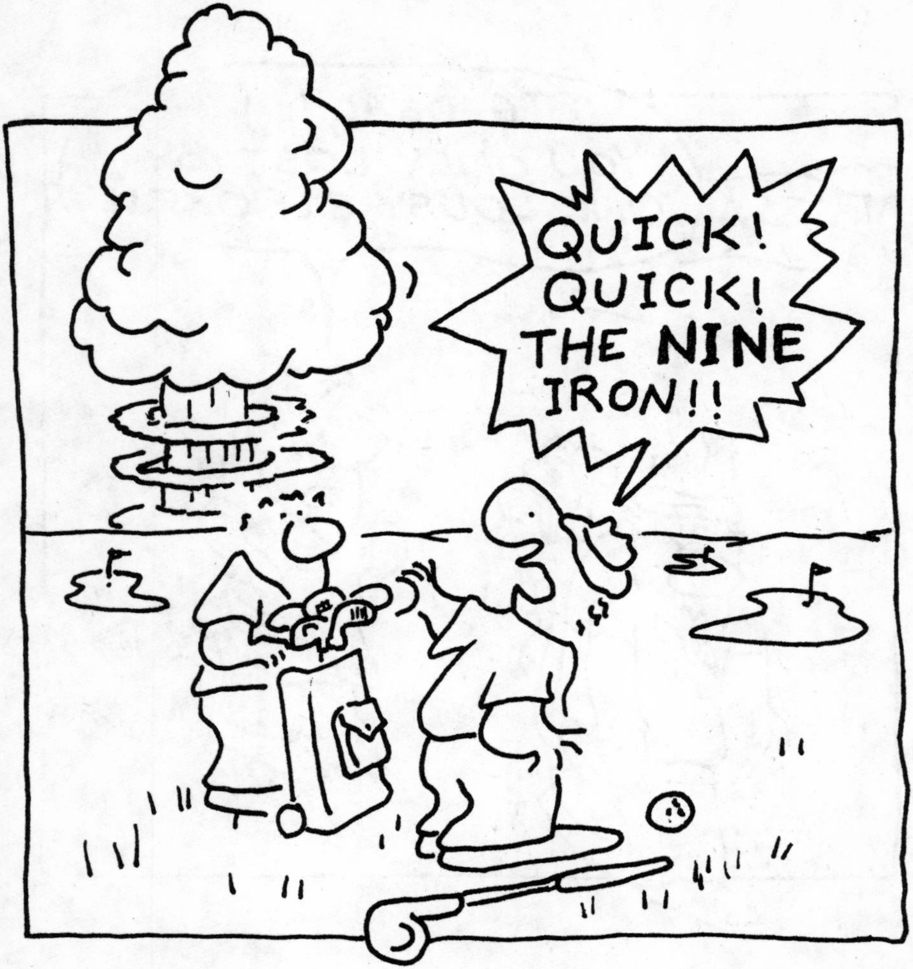
QUICK! QUICK! THE NINE IRON!!

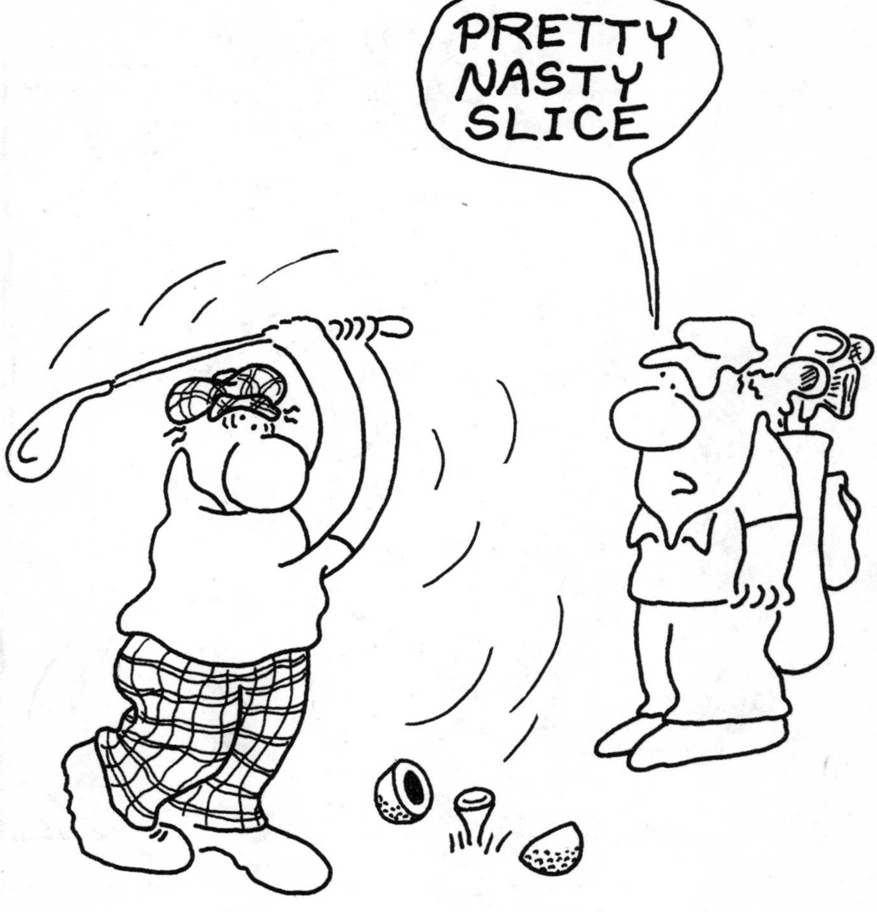
PRETTY NASTY SLICE

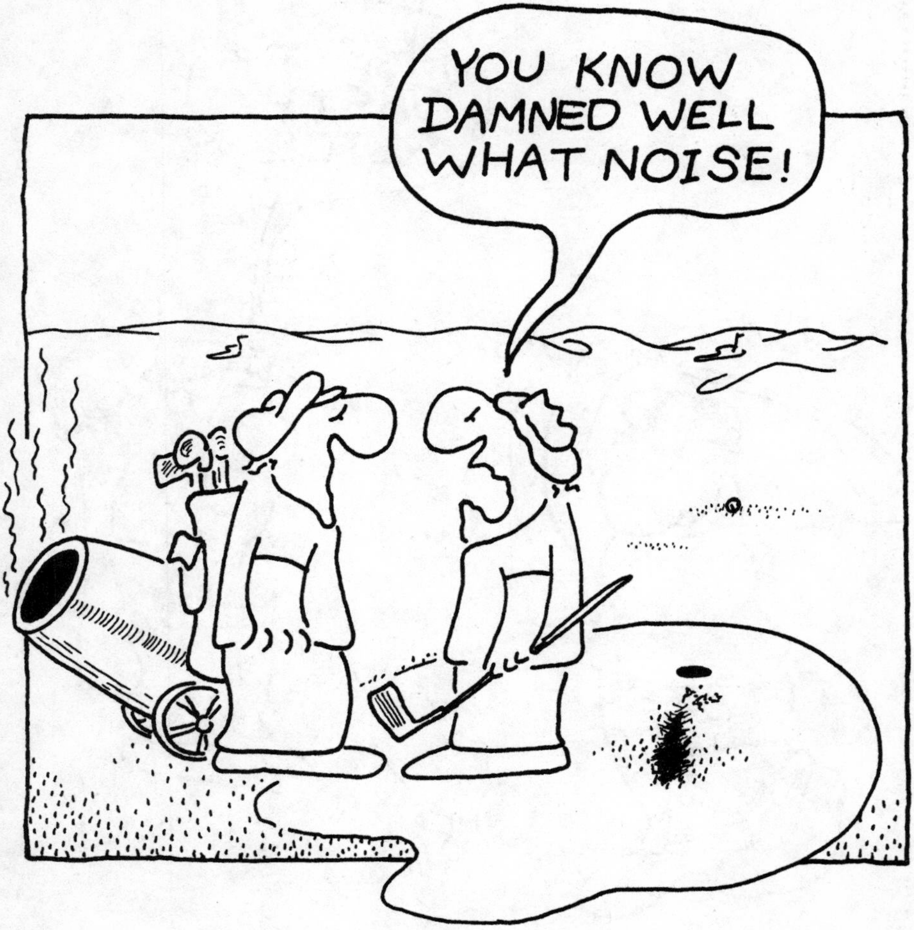
YOU KNOW DAMNED WELL WHAT NOISE!

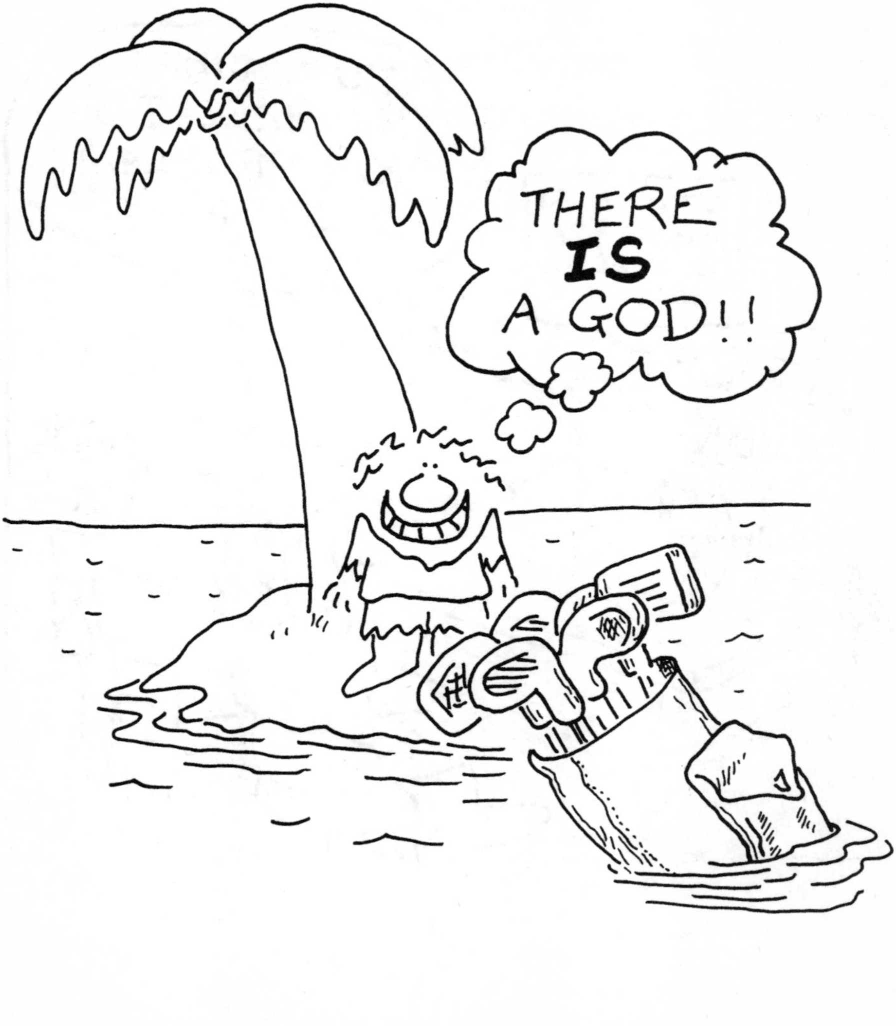
THERE
IS
A GOD!!

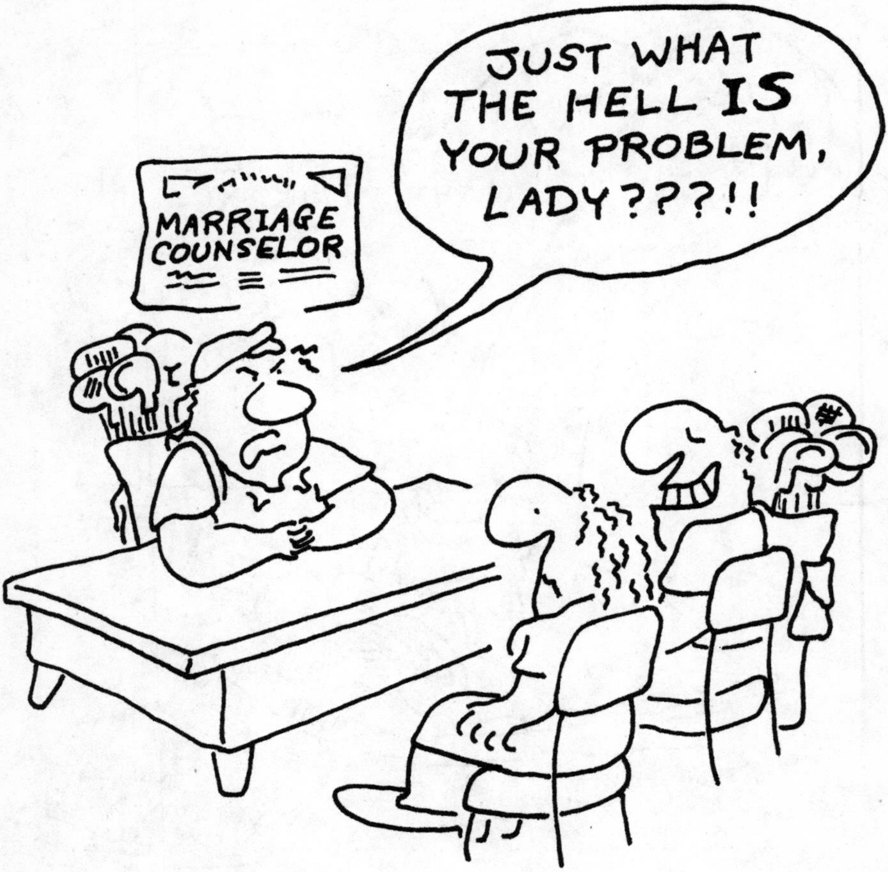
JUST WHAT THE HELL IS YOUR PROBLEM, LADY???!!
MARRIAGE COUNSELOR

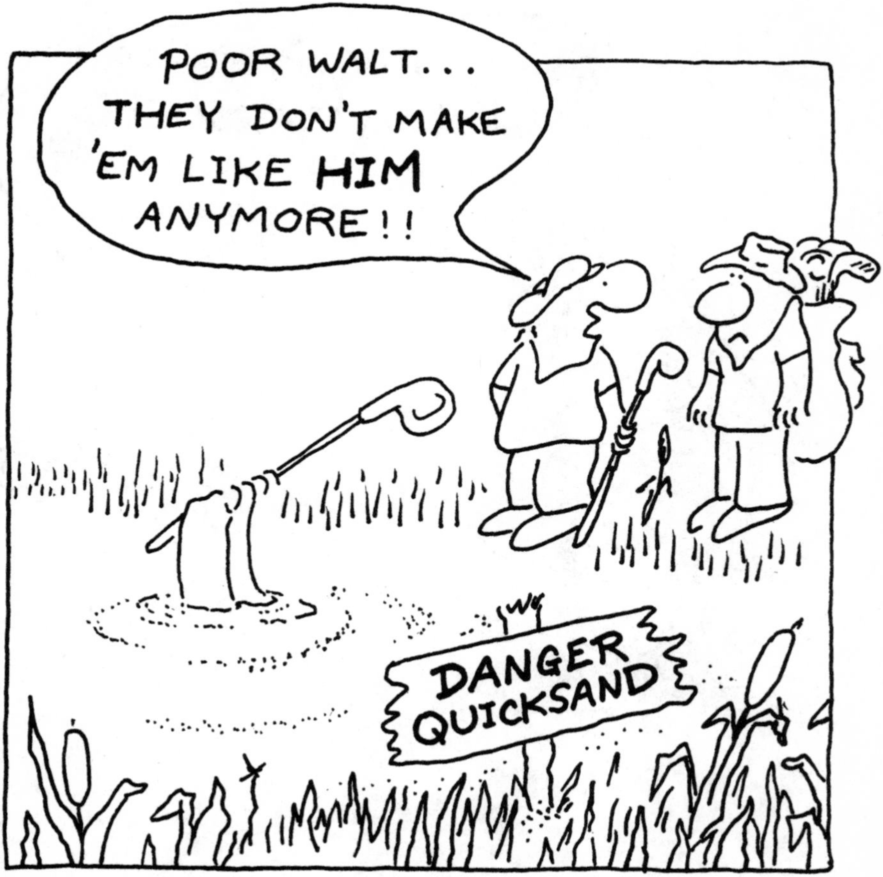
POOR WALT...
THEY DON'T MAKE 'EM LIKE HIM ANYMORE!!
DANGER
QUICKSAND

I HATE GOLF!

BUT I LIKE WEARING
SILLY PANTS

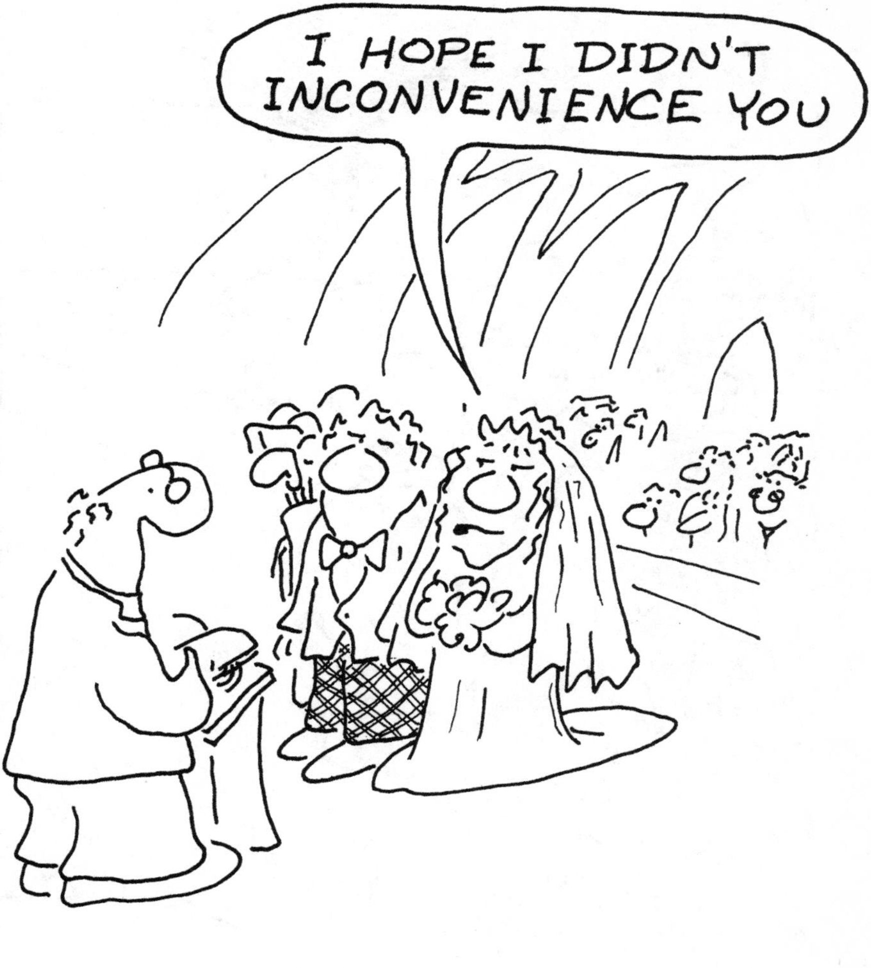
I HOPE I DIDN'T INCONVENIENCE YOU

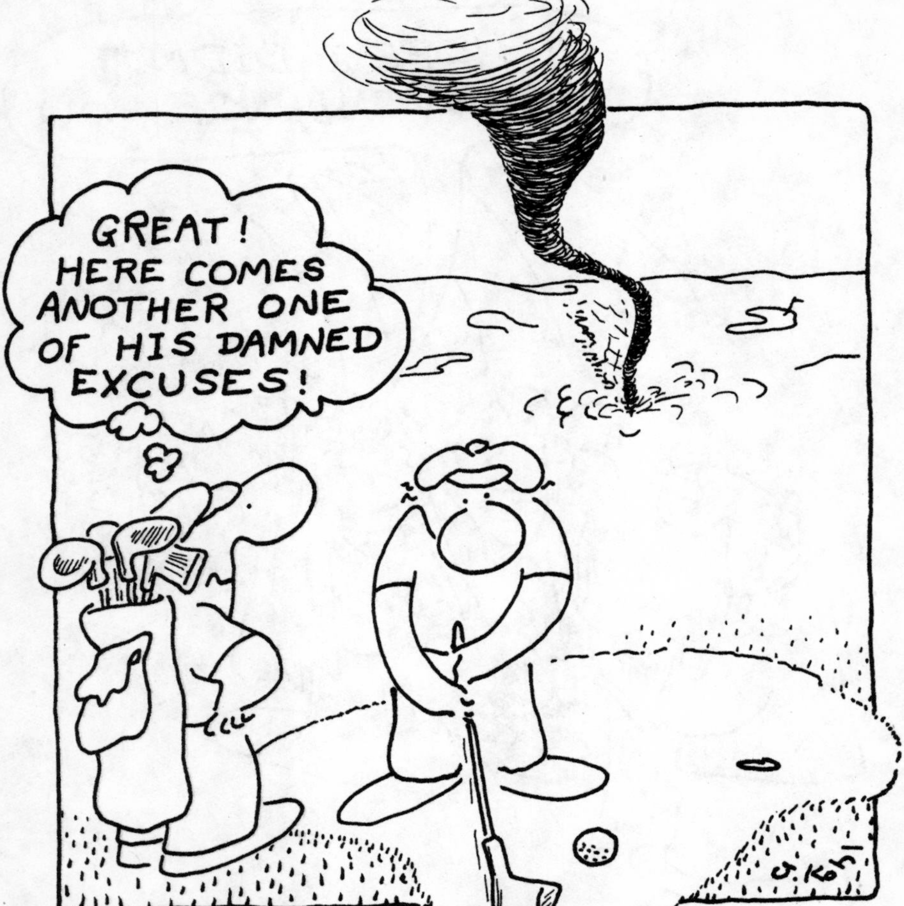
GREAT! HERE COMES ANOTHER ONE OF HIS DAMNED EXCUSES!
J. Koren

GOLF MYTH #203

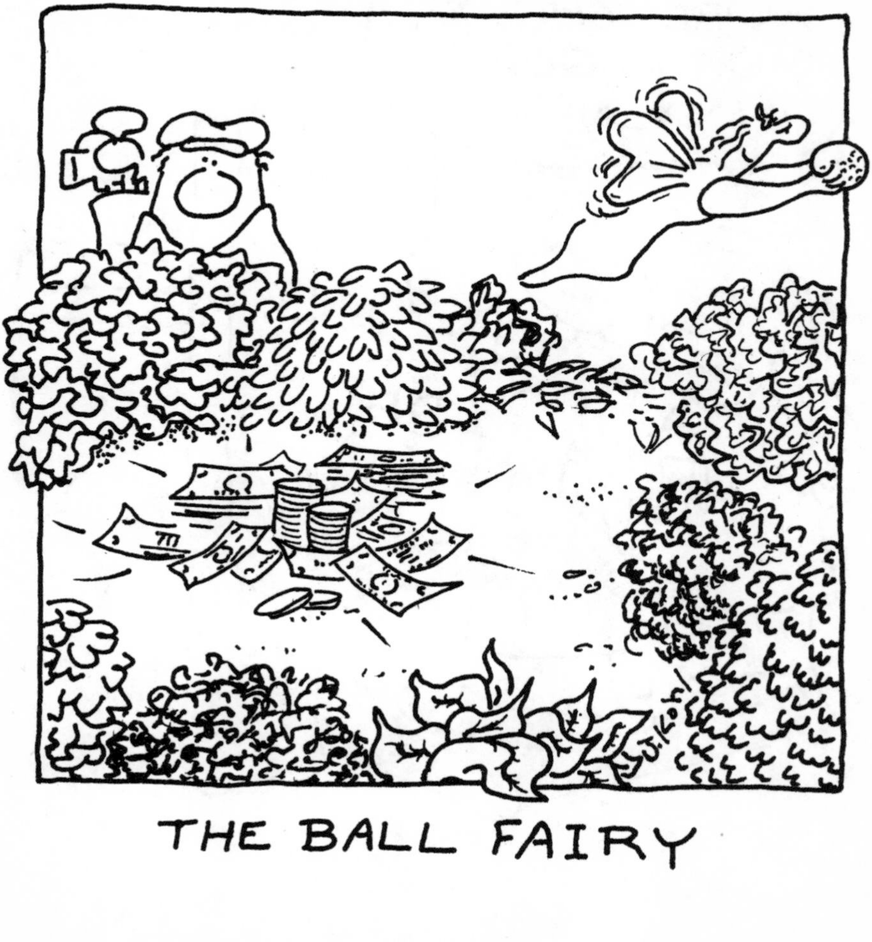

THE BALL FAIRY

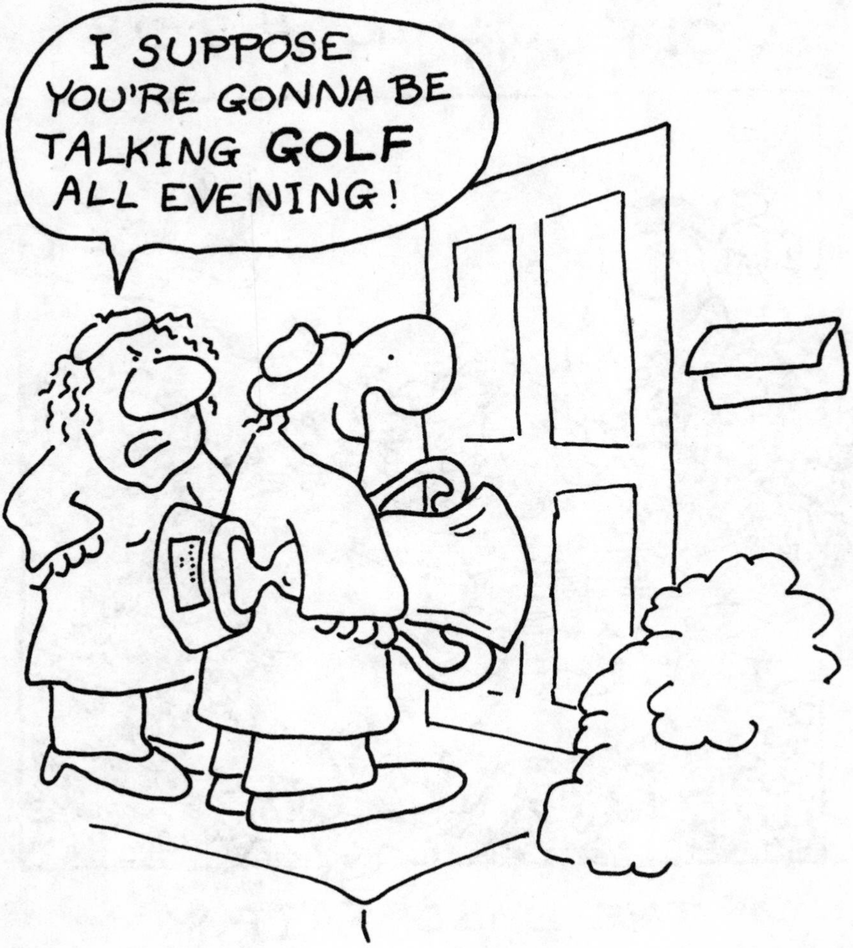
I SUPPOSE YOU'RE GONNA BE TALKING GOLF ALL EVENING!

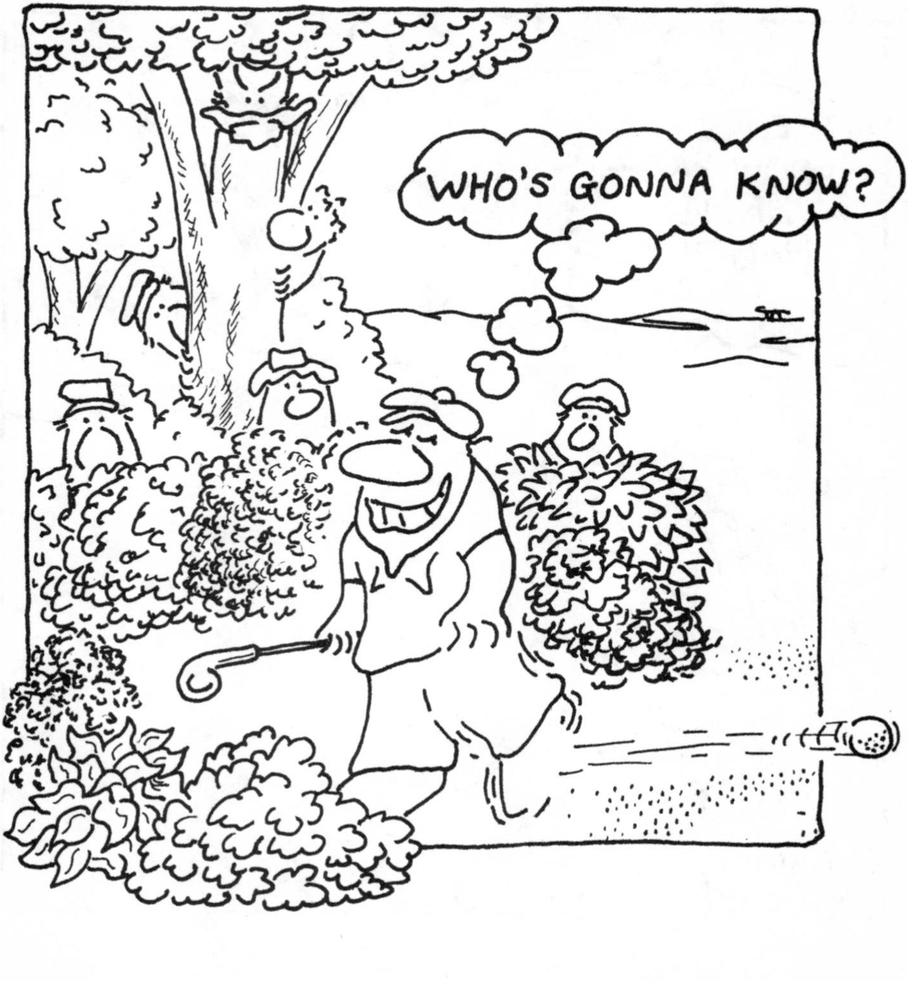
WHO'S GONNA KNOW?

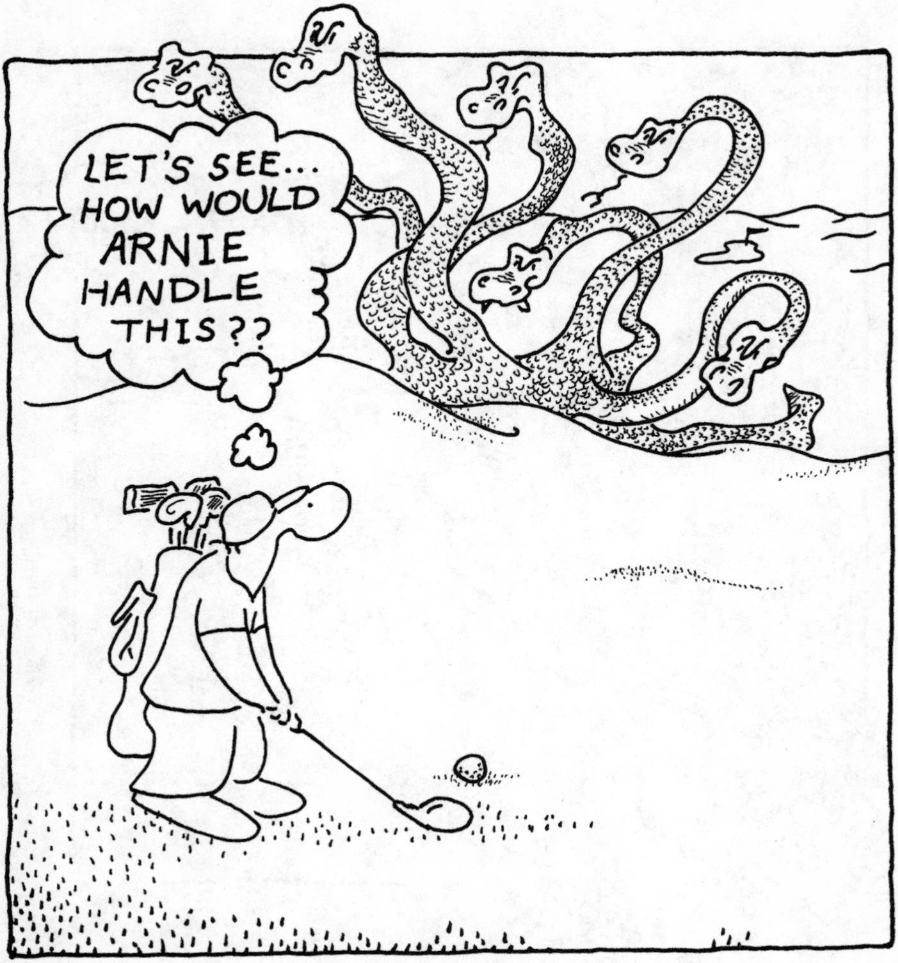
LET'S SEE... HOW WOULD ARNIE HANDLE THIS??

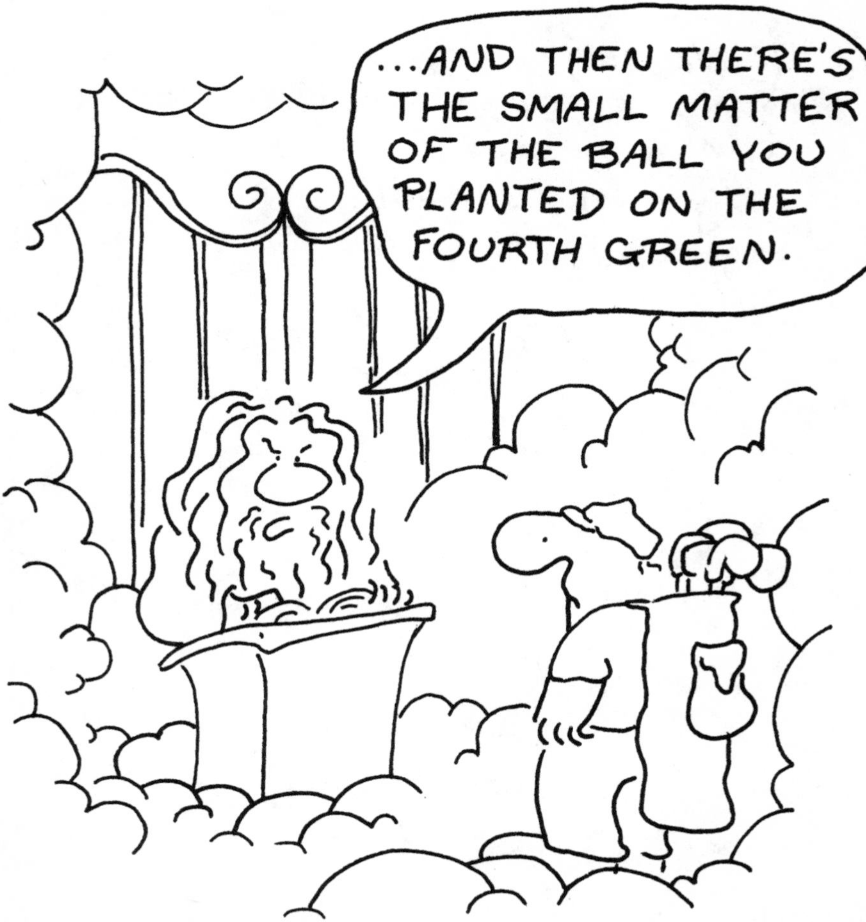
...AND THEN THERE'S THE SMALL MATTER OF THE BALL YOU PLANTED ON THE FOURTH GREEN.

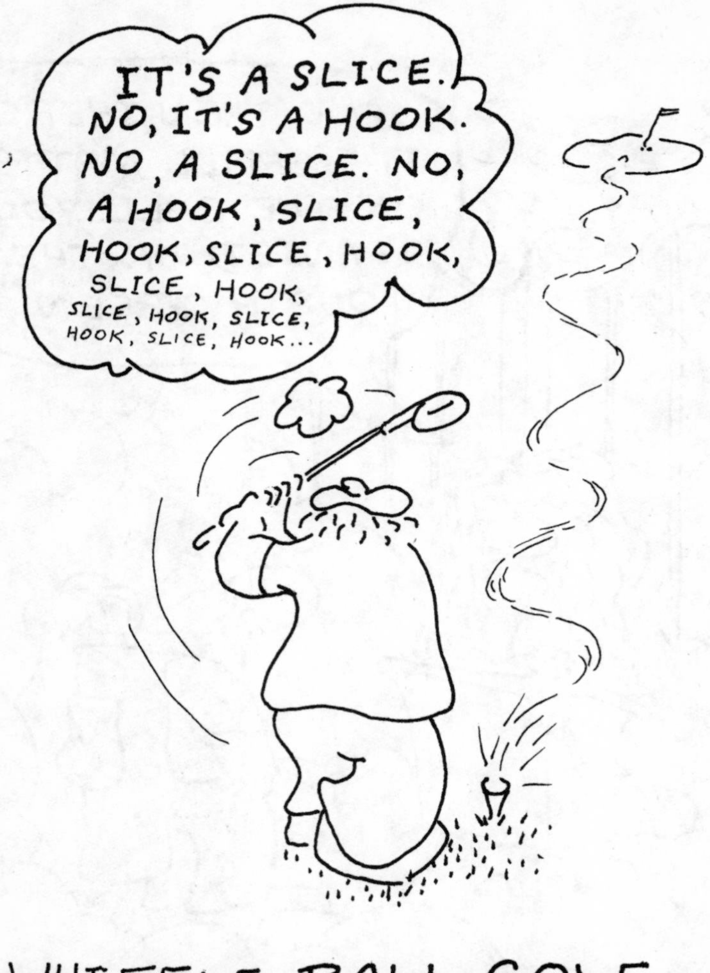
IT'S A SLICE. NO, IT'S A HOOK. NO, A SLICE. NO, A HOOK, SLICE, HOOK, SLICE, HOOK, SLICE, HOOK, SLICE, HOOK, SLICE, HOOK, SLICE, HOOK...

WHIFFLE BALL GOLF

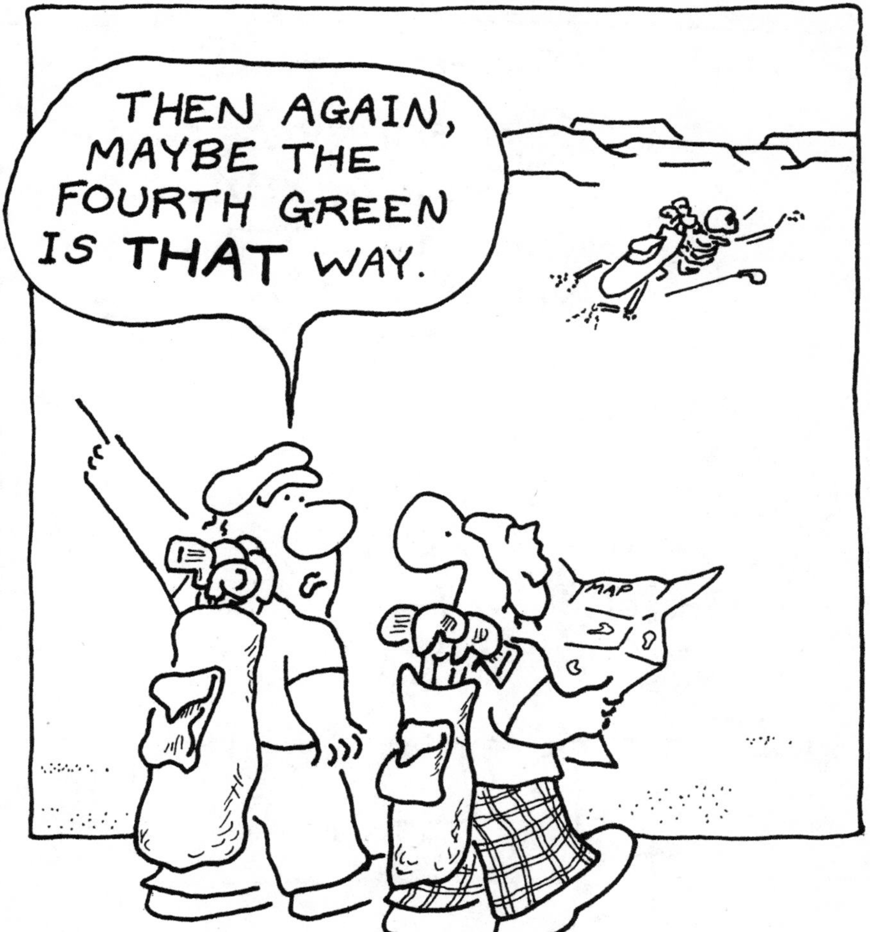
THEN AGAIN, MAYBE THE FOURTH GREEN IS THAT WAY.
MAP

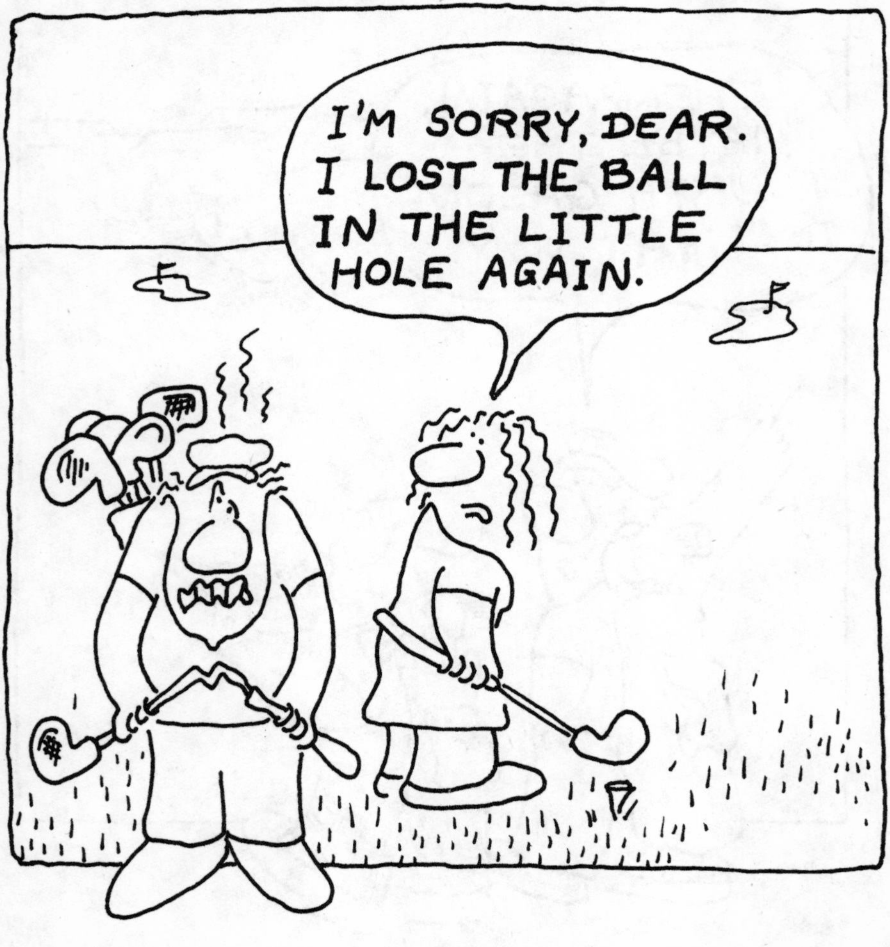
I'M SORRY, DEAR. I LOST THE BALL IN THE LITTLE HOLE AGAIN.

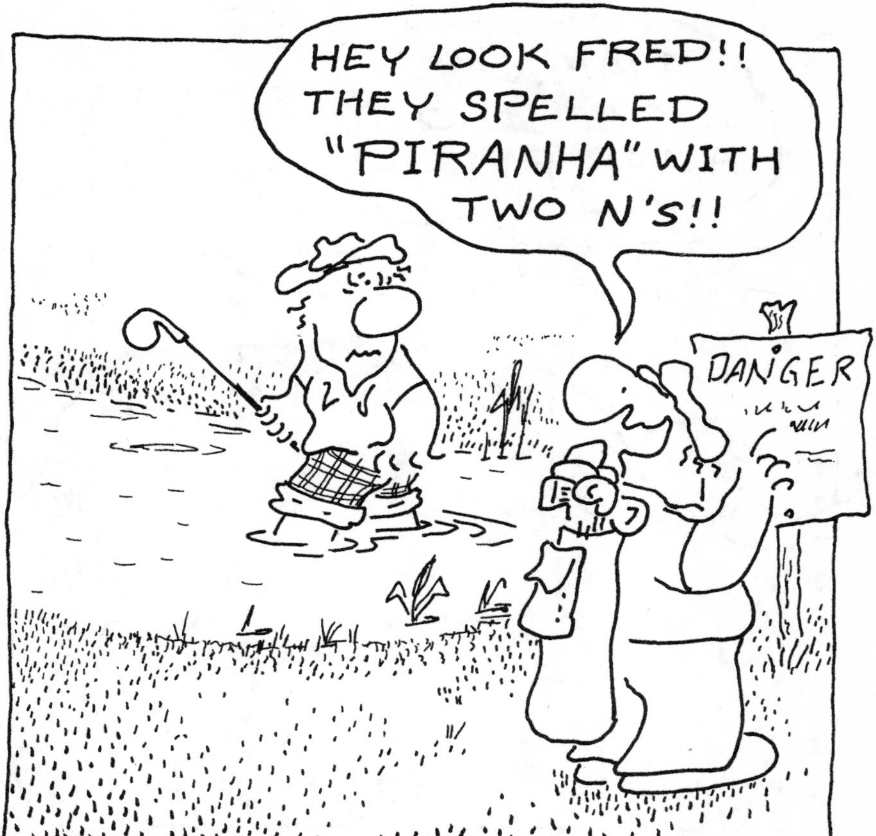
HEY LOOK FRED!! THEY SPELLED "PIRANHA" WITH TWO N'S!!
DANIGER

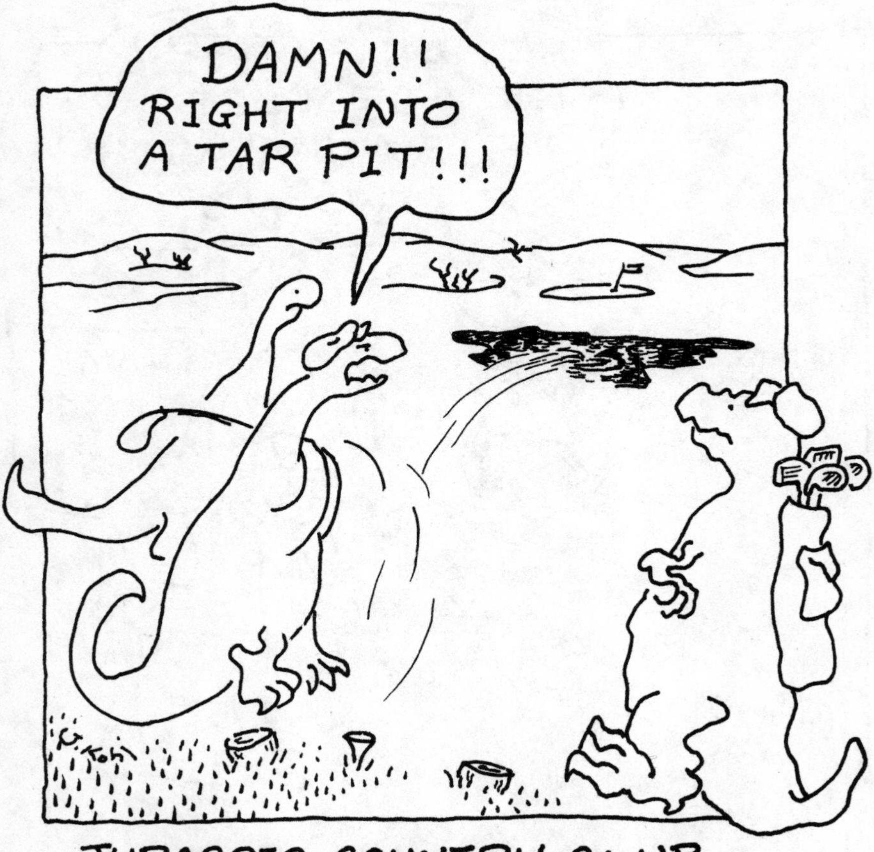
DAMN!! RIGHT INTO A TAR PIT!!!
G. Koh

JURASSIC COUNTRY CLUB

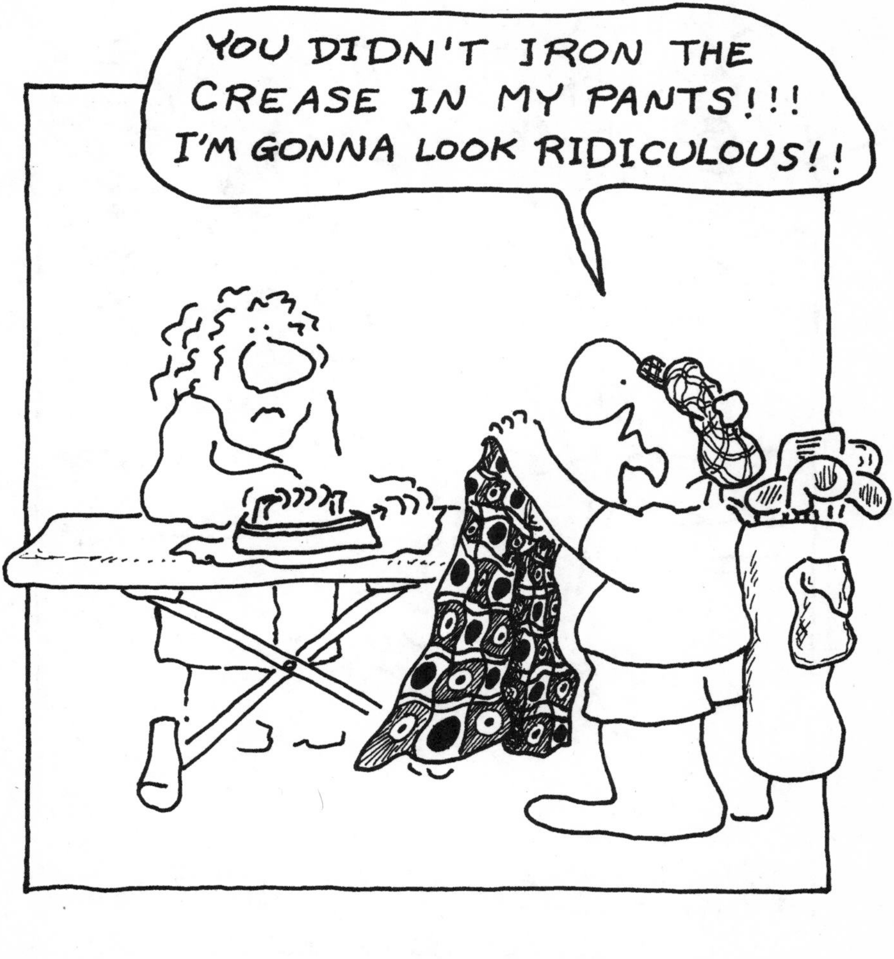
YOU DIDN'T IRON THE CREASE IN MY PANTS!!! I'M GONNA LOOK RIDICULOUS!!

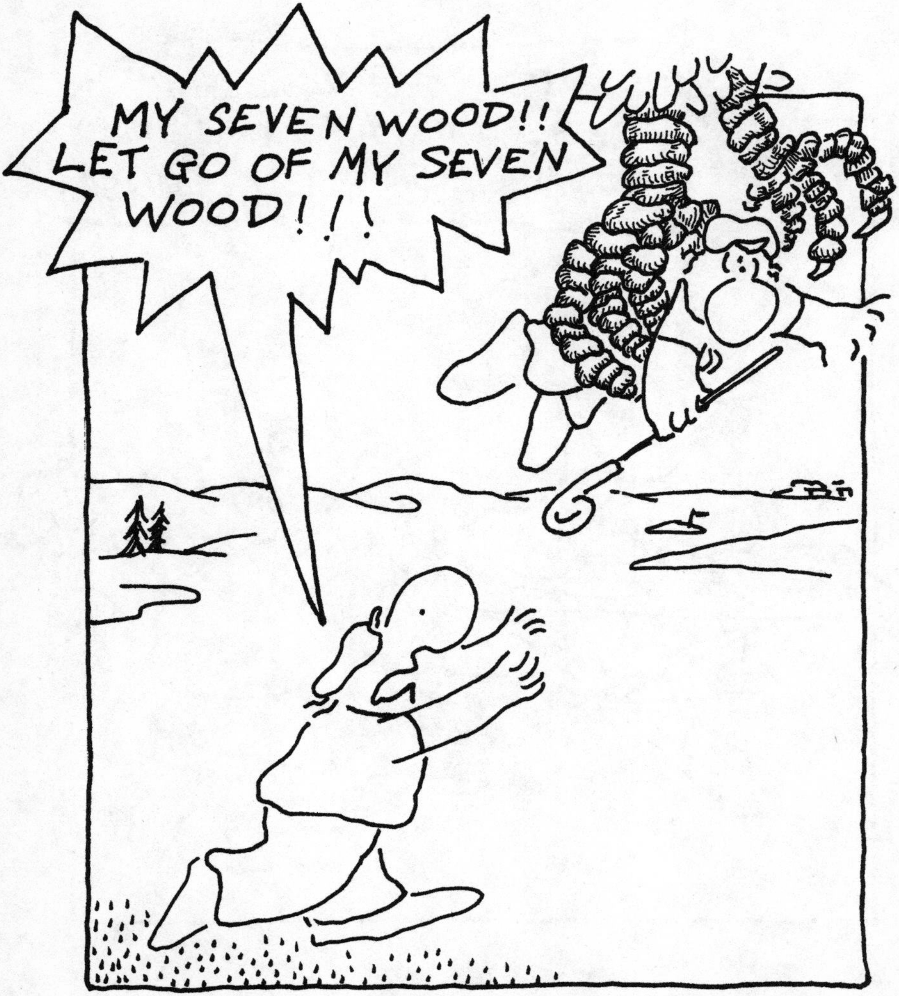
MY SEVEN WOOD!! LET GO OF MY SEVEN WOOD!!!

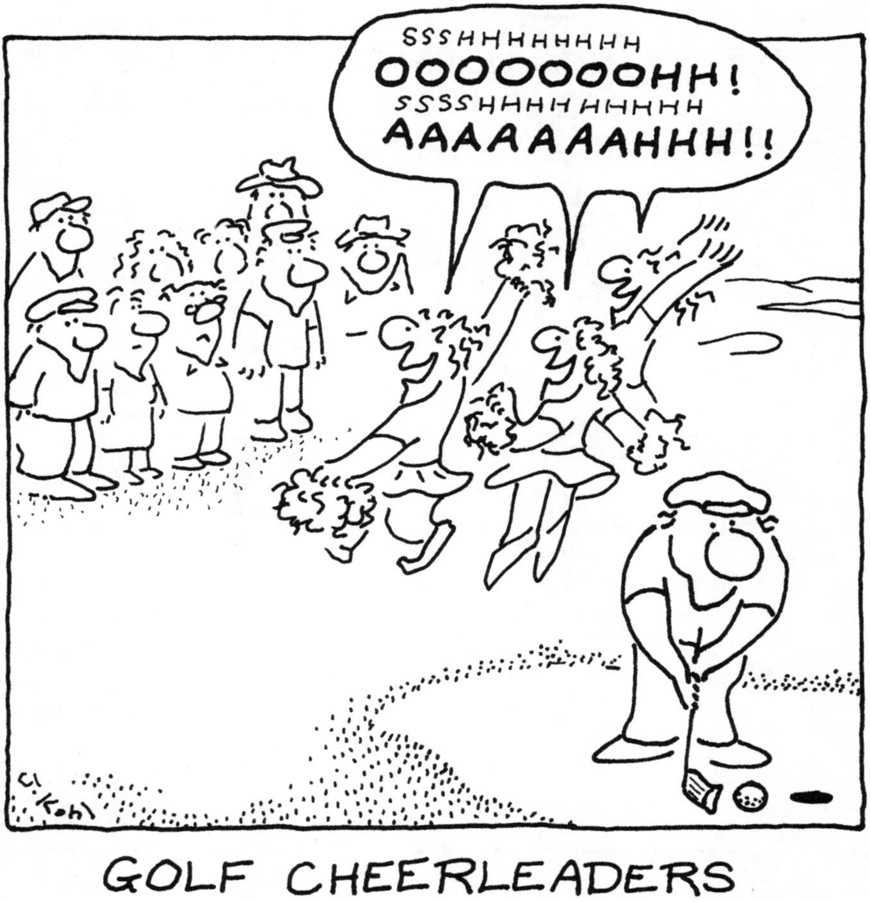
SSSHHHHHHHH
OOOOOOOHH!
SSSSHHHHHHHHH
AAAAAAAHHH!!

GOLF CHEERLEADERS

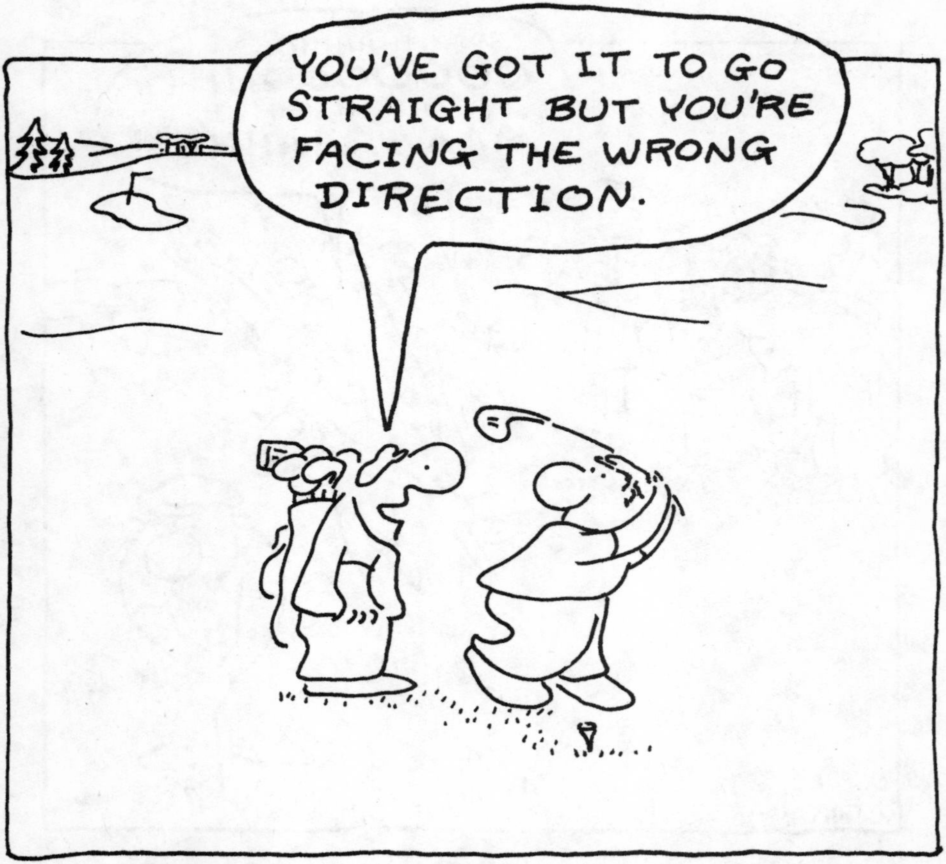
YOU'VE GOT IT TO GO STRAIGHT BUT YOU'RE FACING THE WRONG DIRECTION.

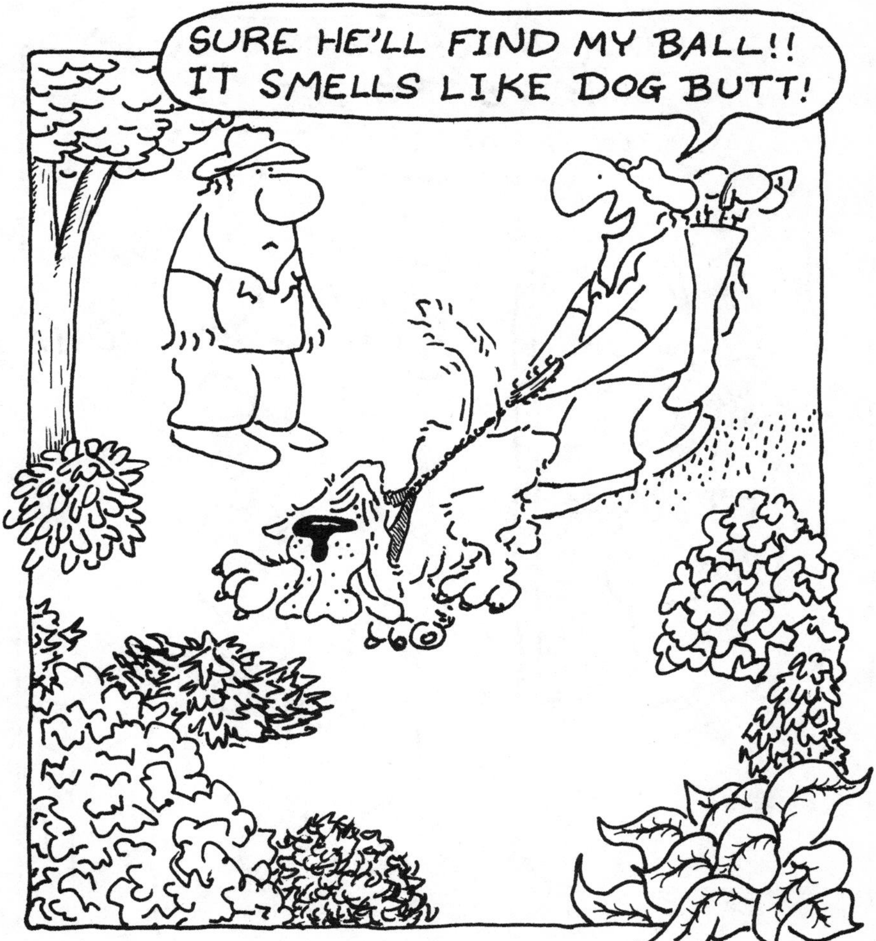
SURE HE'LL FIND MY BALL!! IT SMELLS LIKE DOG BUTT!

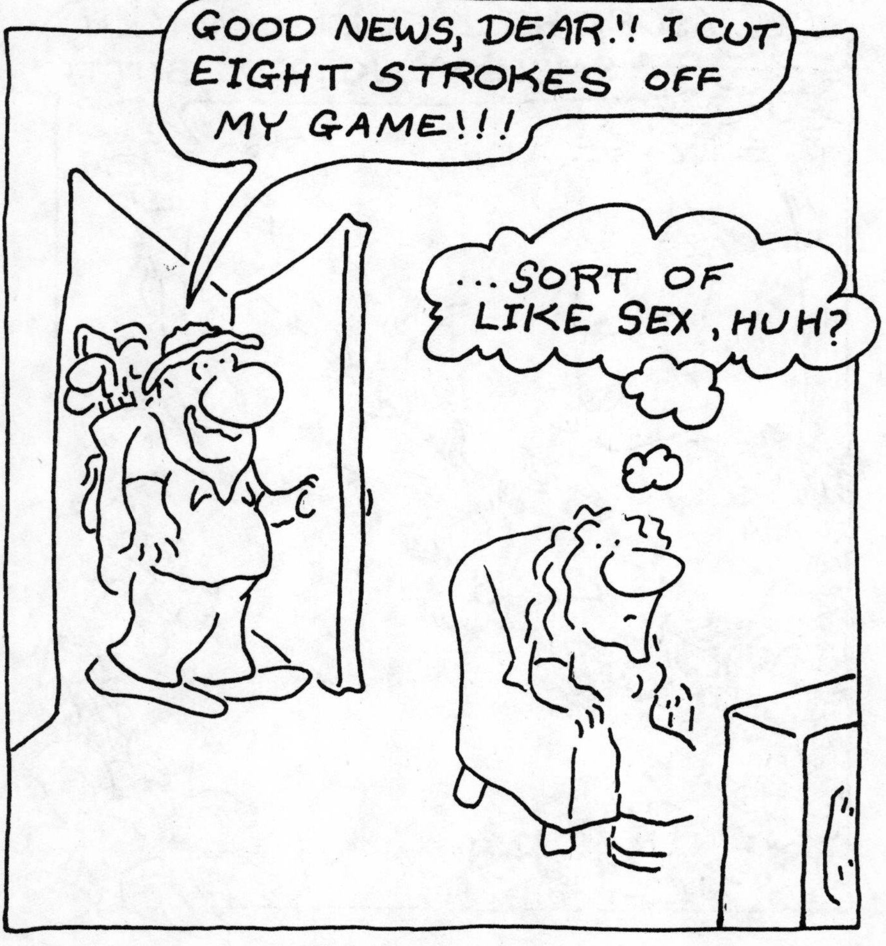
GOOD NEWS, DEAR!! I CUT EIGHT STROKES OFF MY GAME!!!
...SORT OF LIKE SEX, HUH?

GOLF MYTH #278

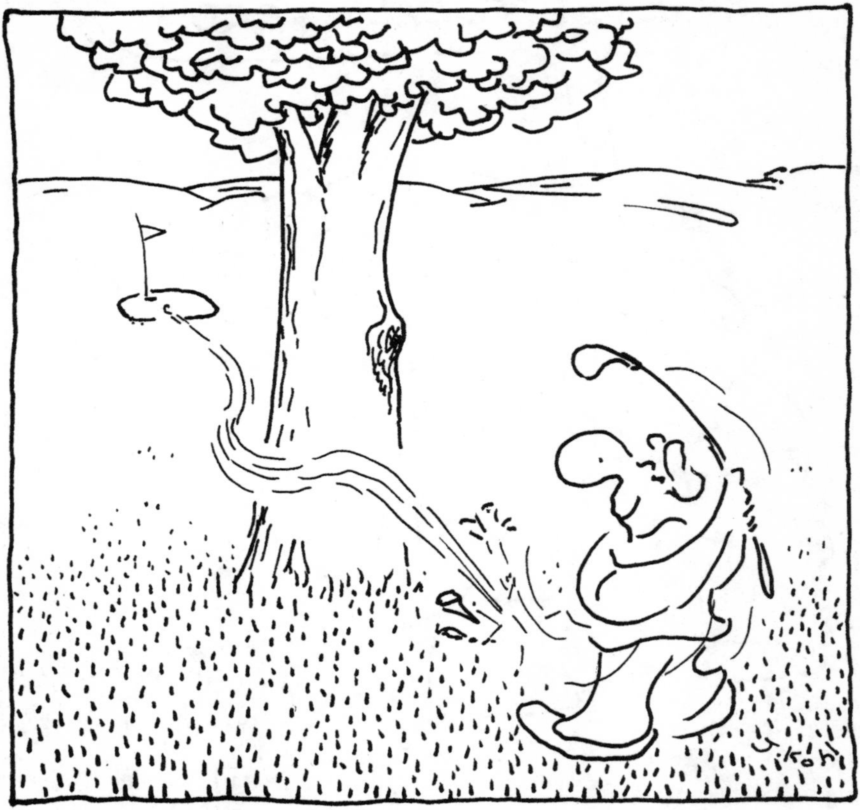
J. Kohl

THAT "SPECIAL" CLUB

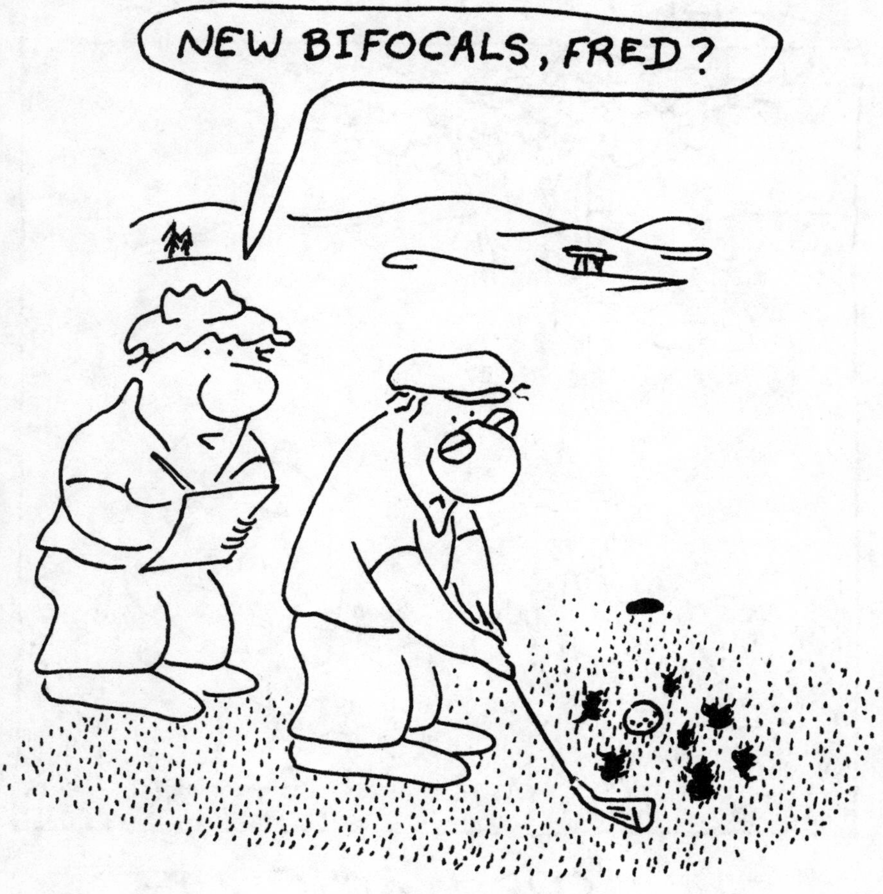
NEW BIFOCALS, FRED?

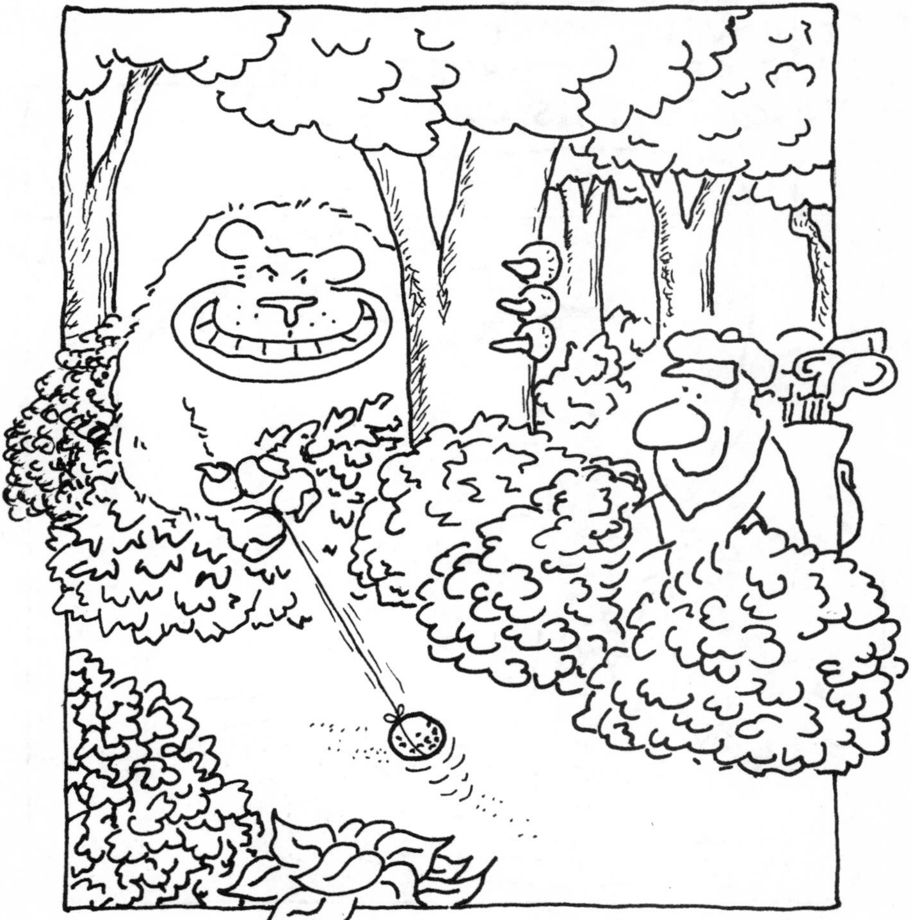

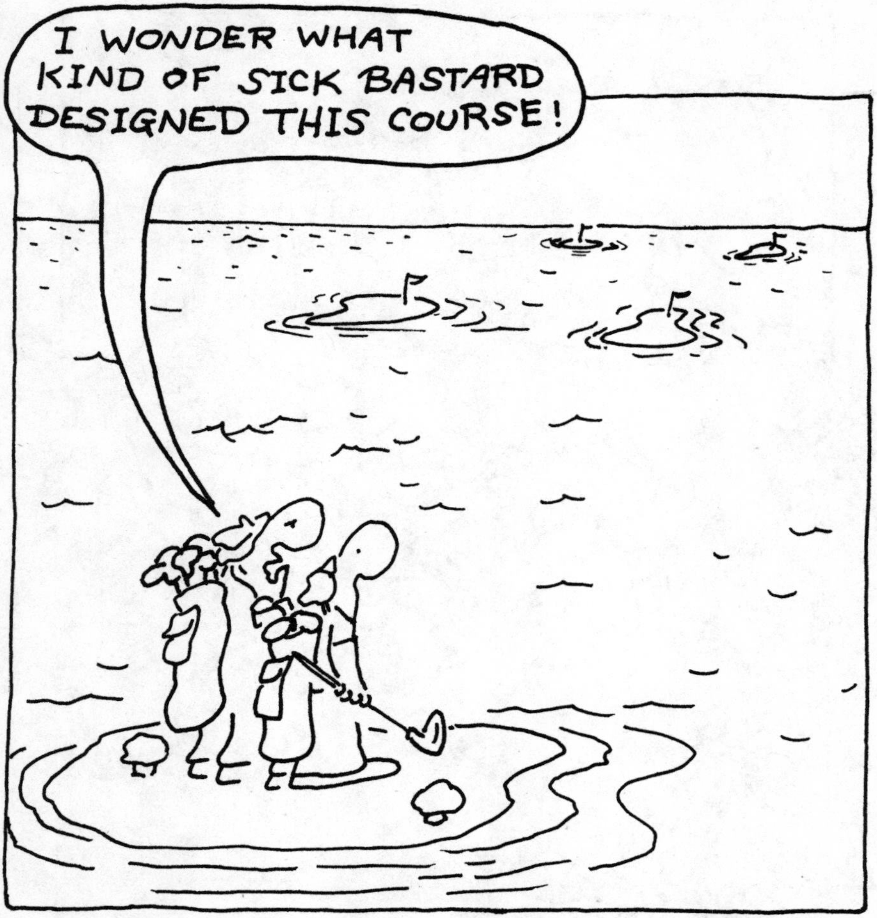
I WONDER WHAT KIND OF SICK BASTARD DESIGNED THIS COURSE!

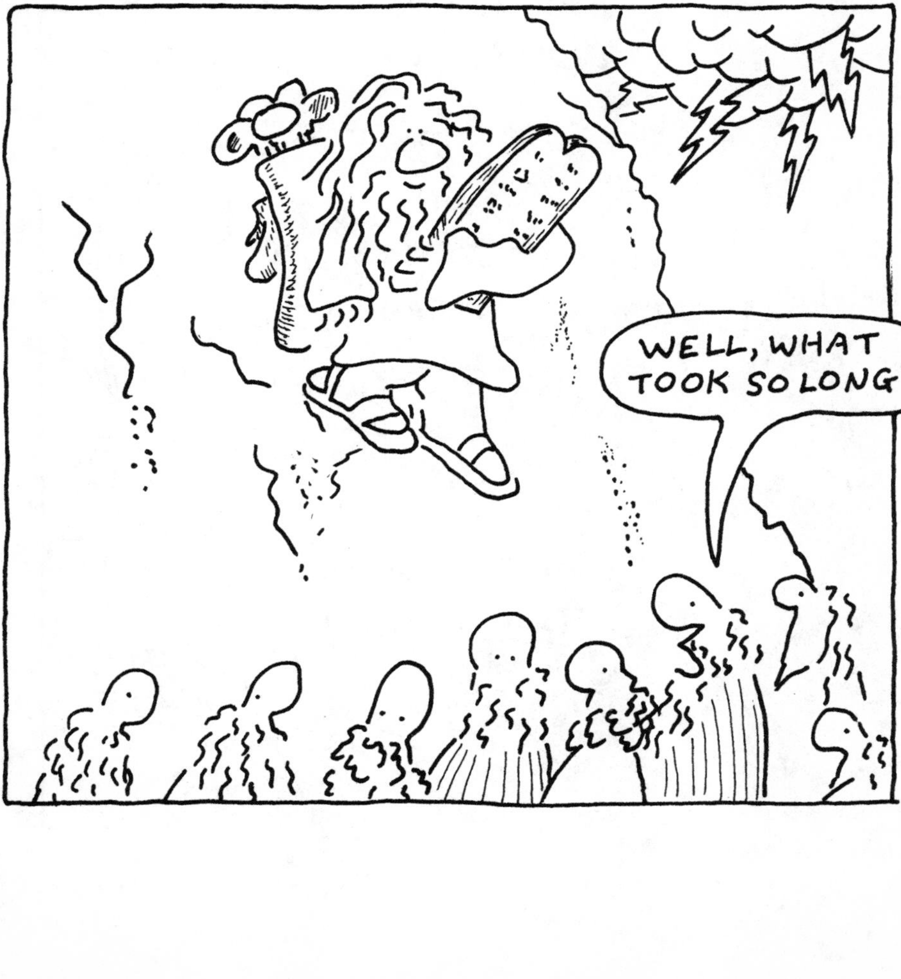
WELL, WHAT TOOK SO LONG?

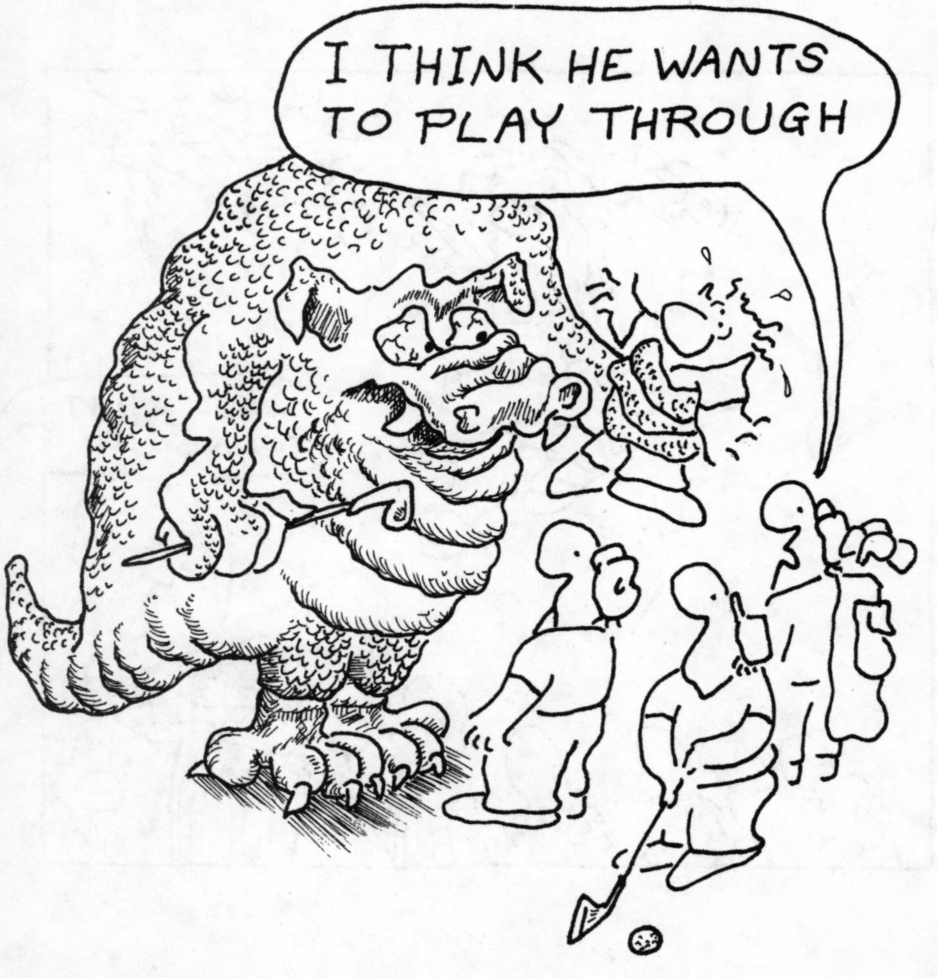
I THINK HE WANTS TO PLAY THROUGH

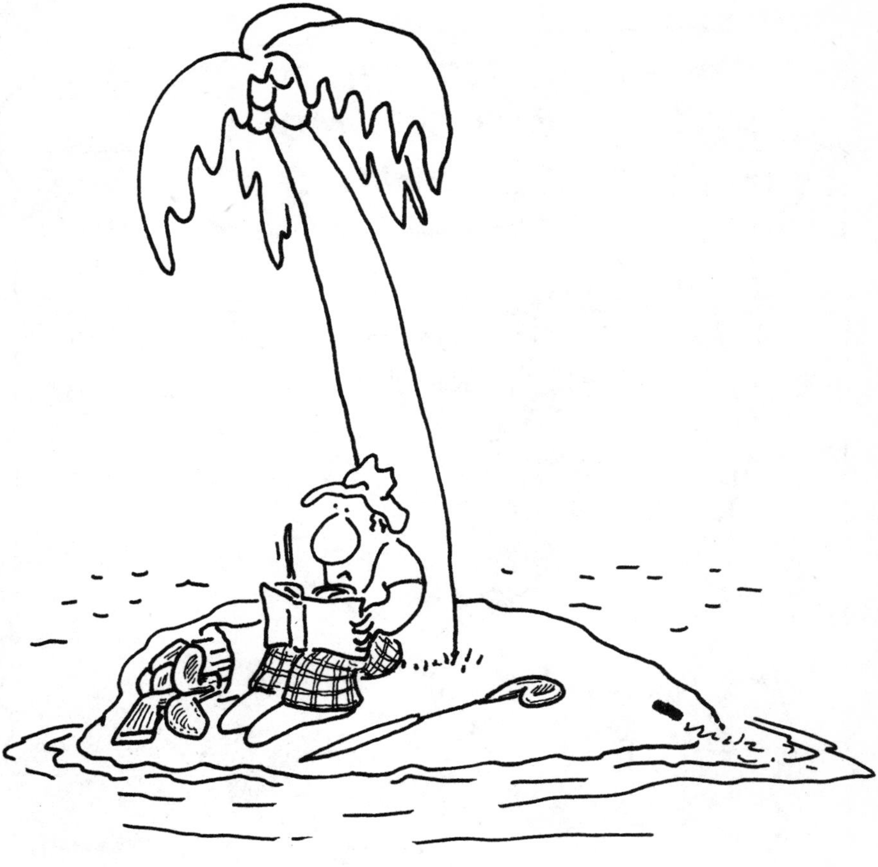

Dear Diary,
Gave up golf.

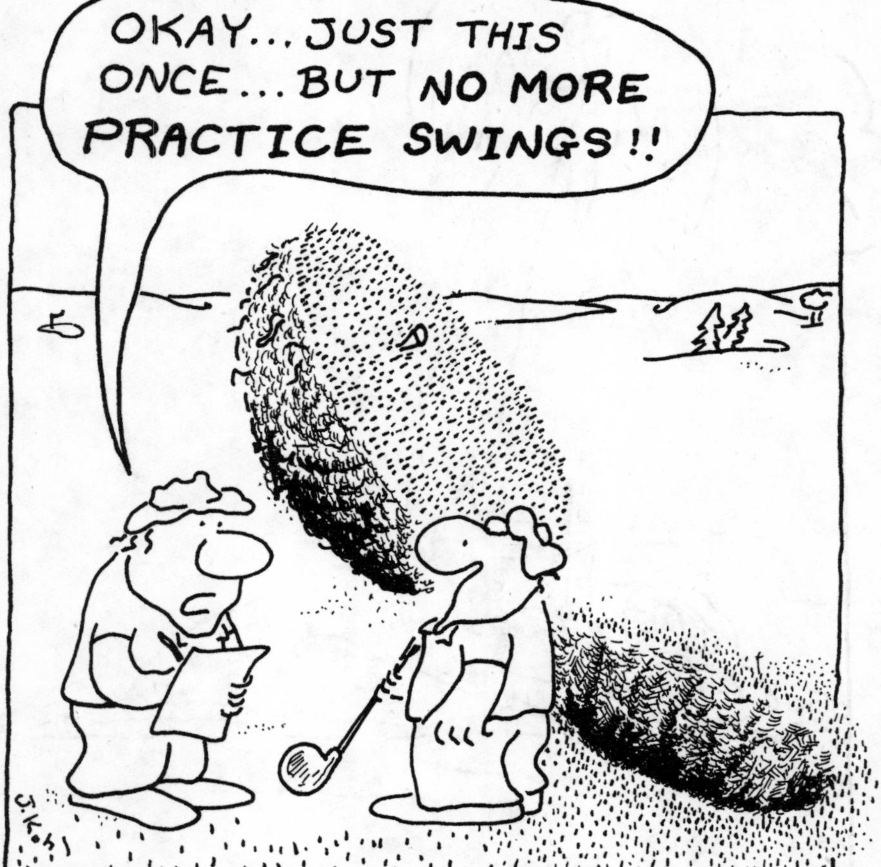
OKAY... JUST THIS ONCE... BUT NO MORE PRACTICE SWINGS!!
J.K.

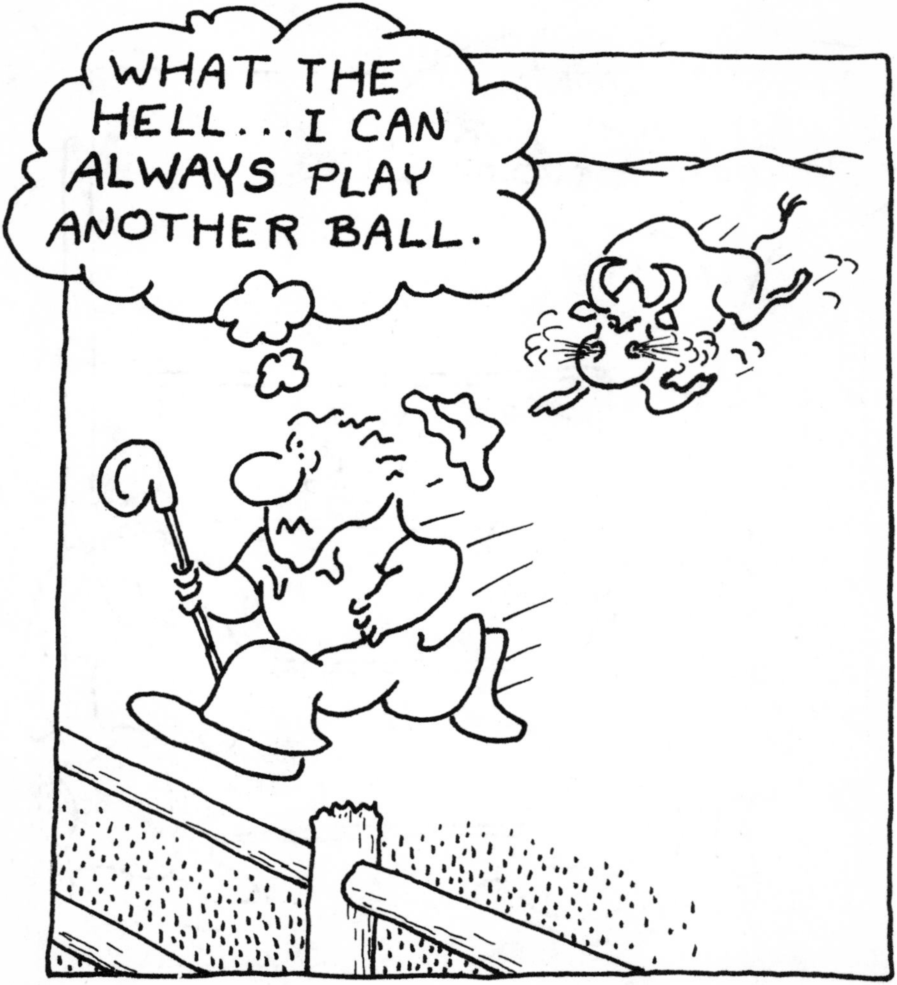
WHAT THE HELL...I CAN ALWAYS PLAY ANOTHER BALL.

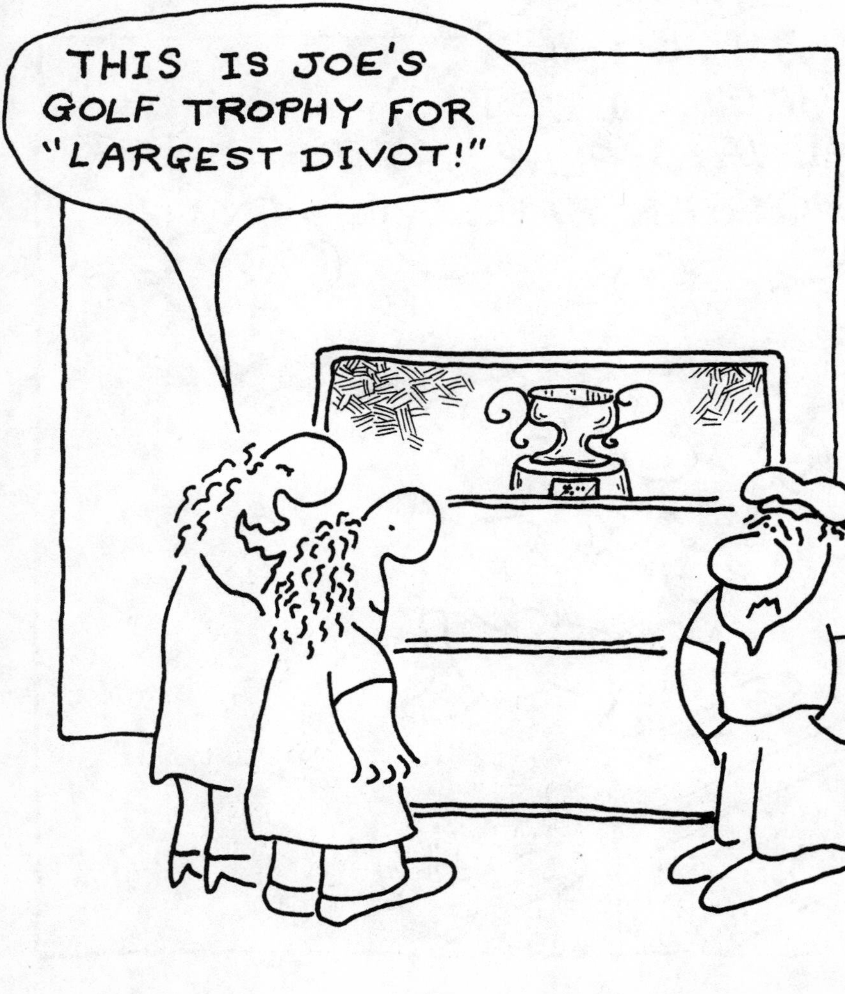
THIS IS JOE'S GOLF TROPHY FOR "LARGEST DIVOT!"

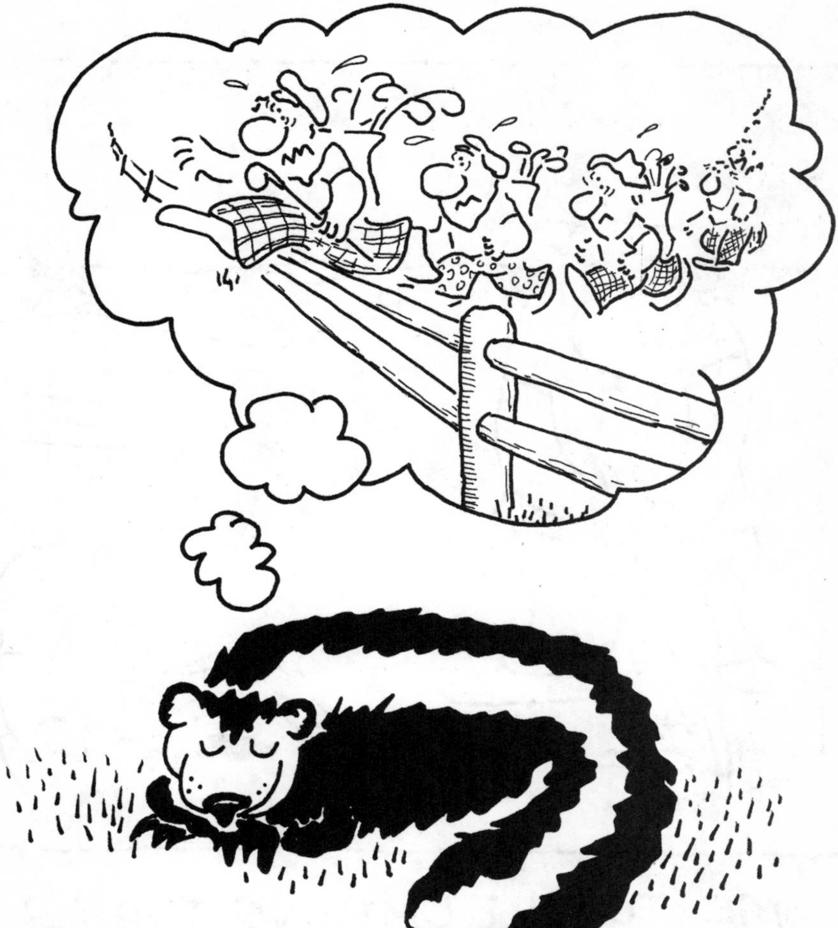

MEXICAN JUMPING BALLS

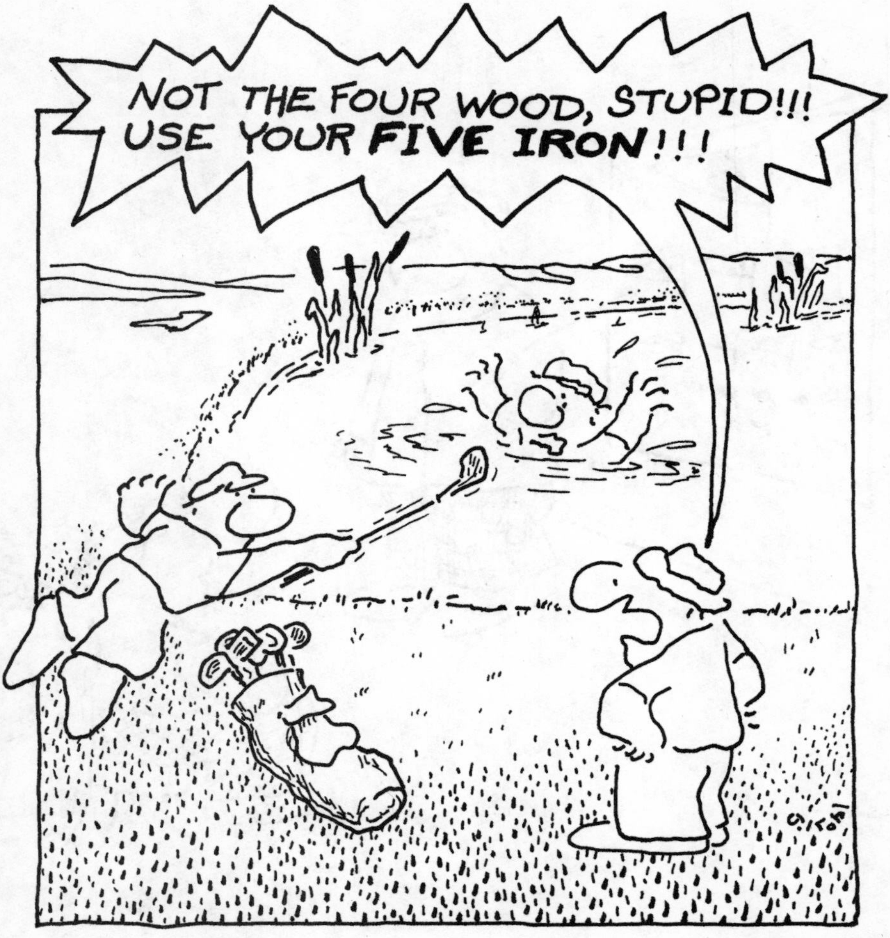
NOT THE FOUR WOOD, STUPID!!!
USE YOUR FIVE IRON!!!

WHERE GOLFERS COME FROM

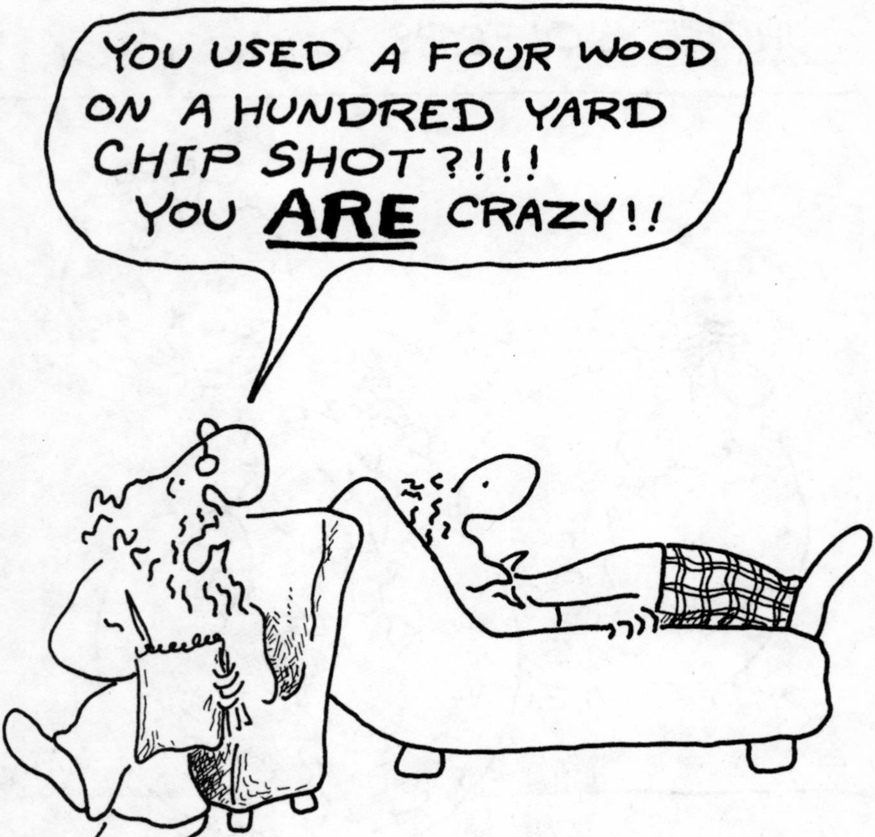
YOU USED A FOUR WOOD ON A HUNDRED YARD CHIP SHOT?!!! YOU ARE CRAZY!!

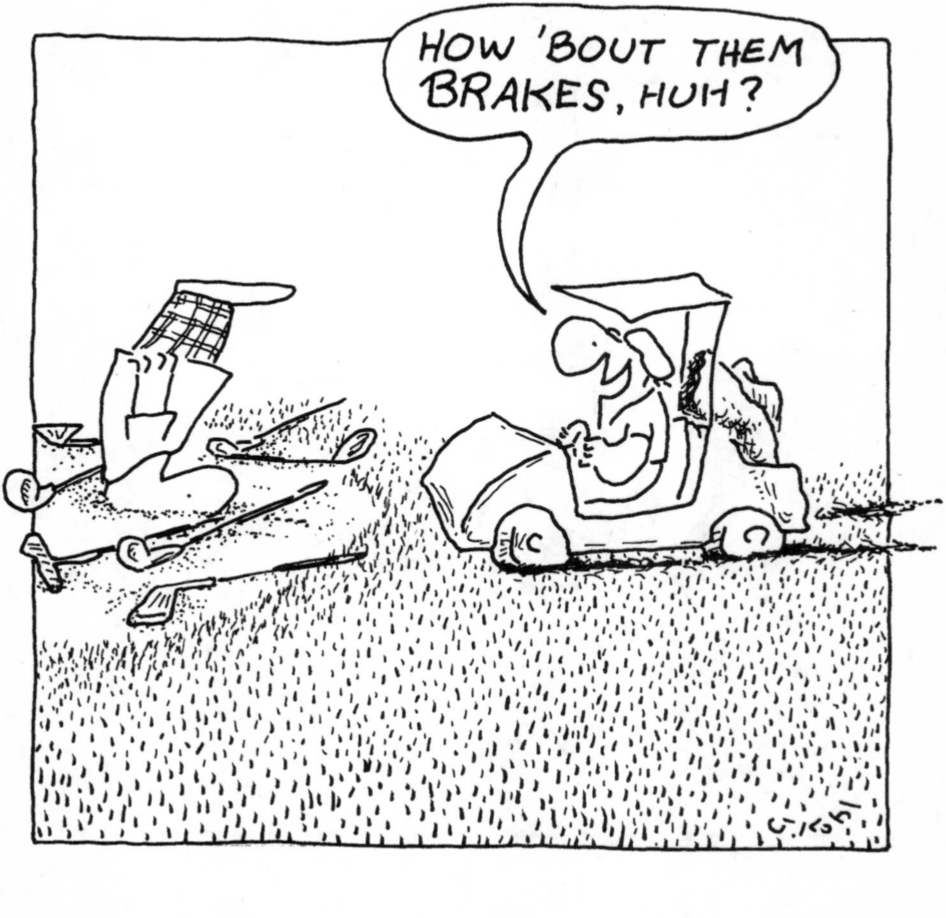
HOW 'BOUT THEM BRAKES, HUH?
C. Kohl

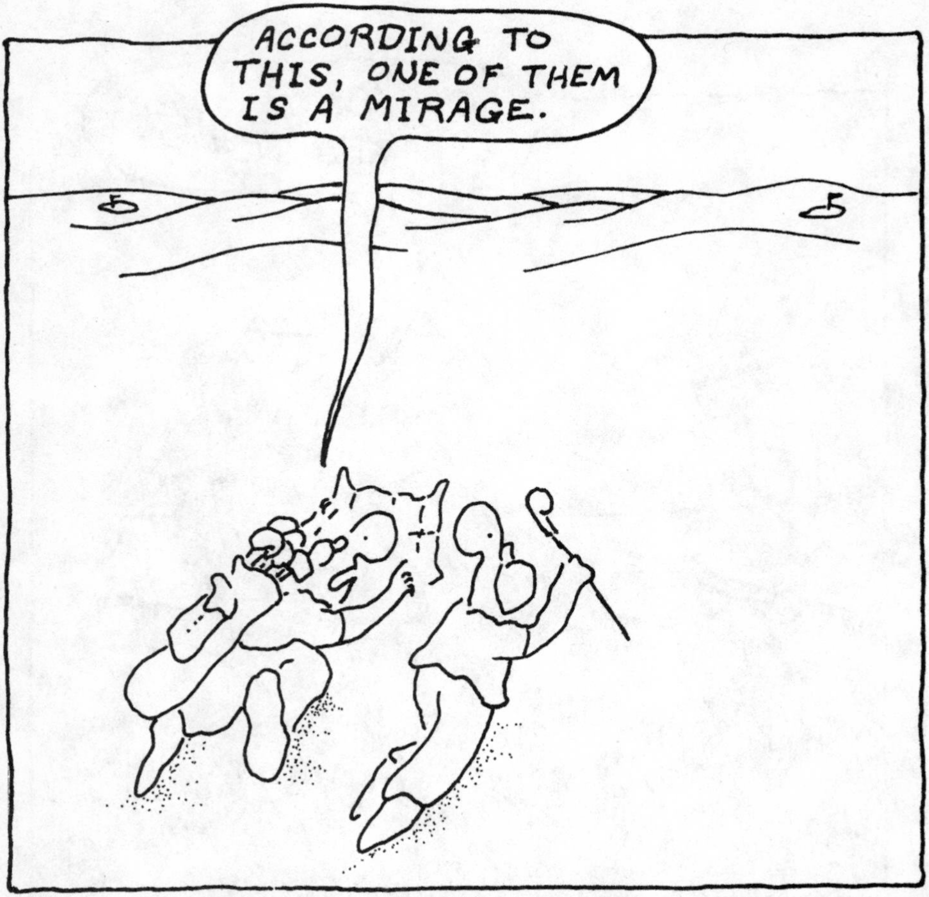
ACCORDING TO THIS, ONE OF THEM IS A MIRAGE.

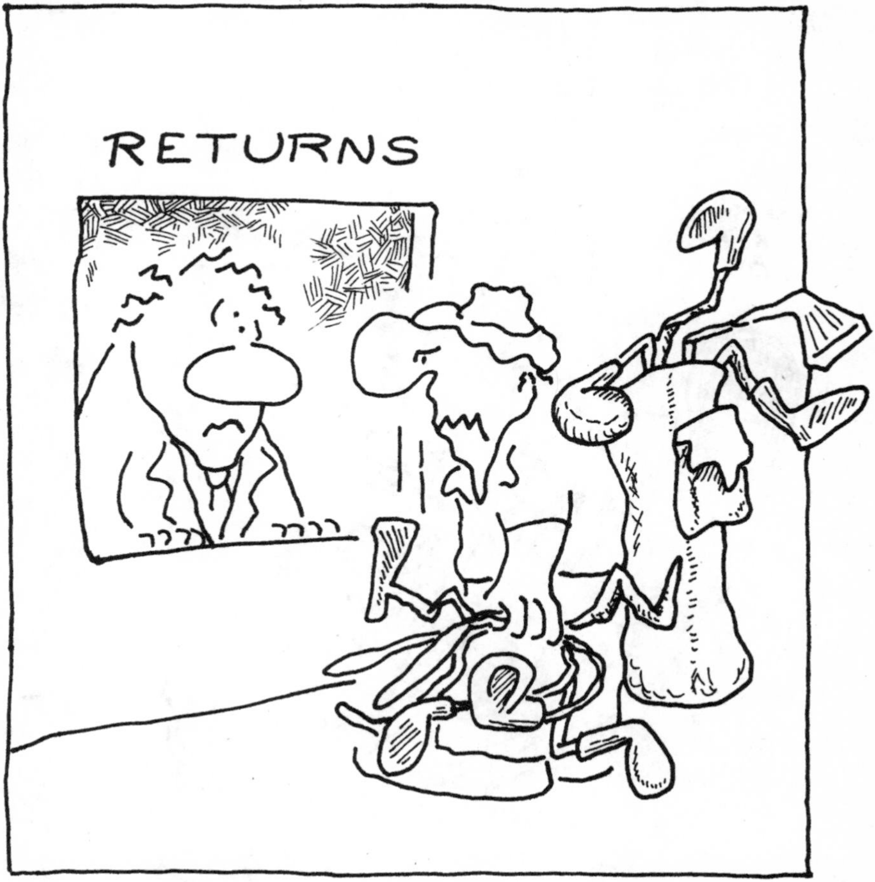
RETURNS

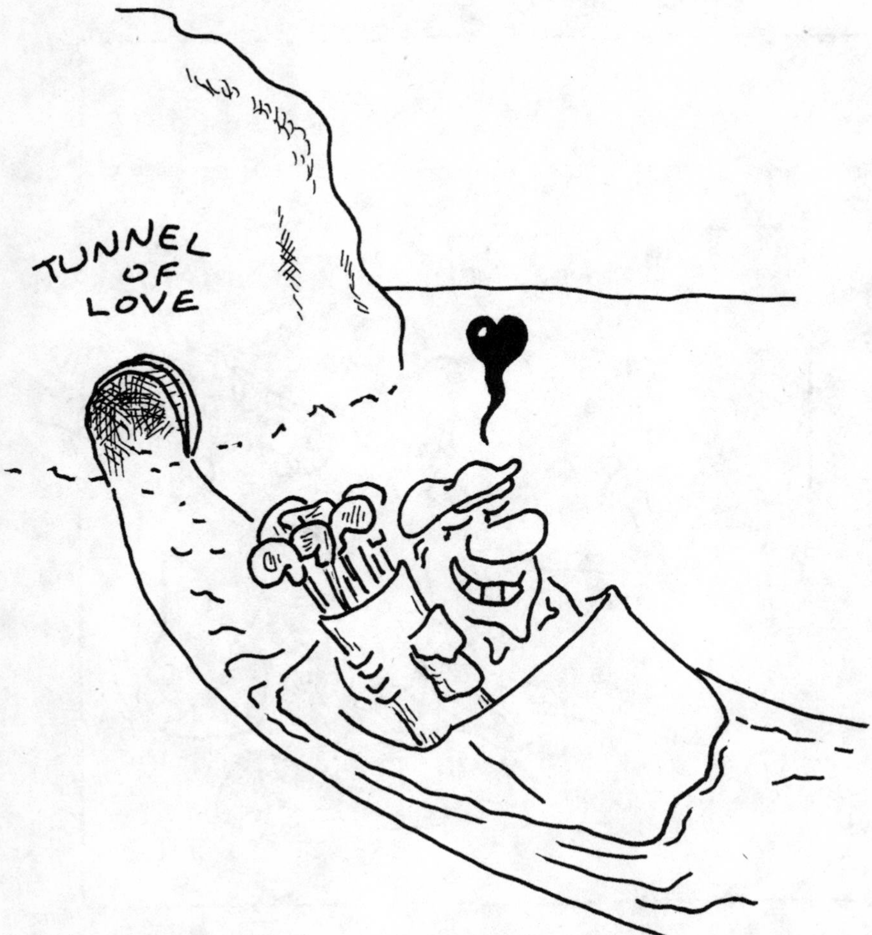
TUNNEL
OF
LOVE

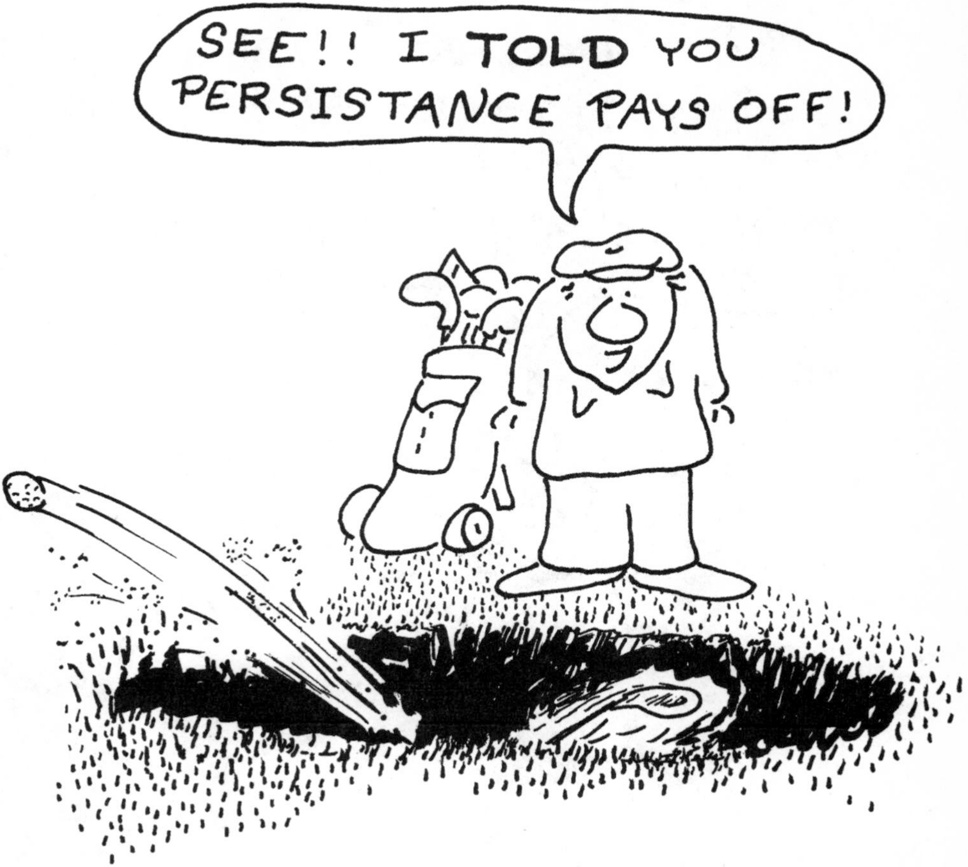
SEE!! I TOLD YOU PERSISTANCE PAYS OFF!

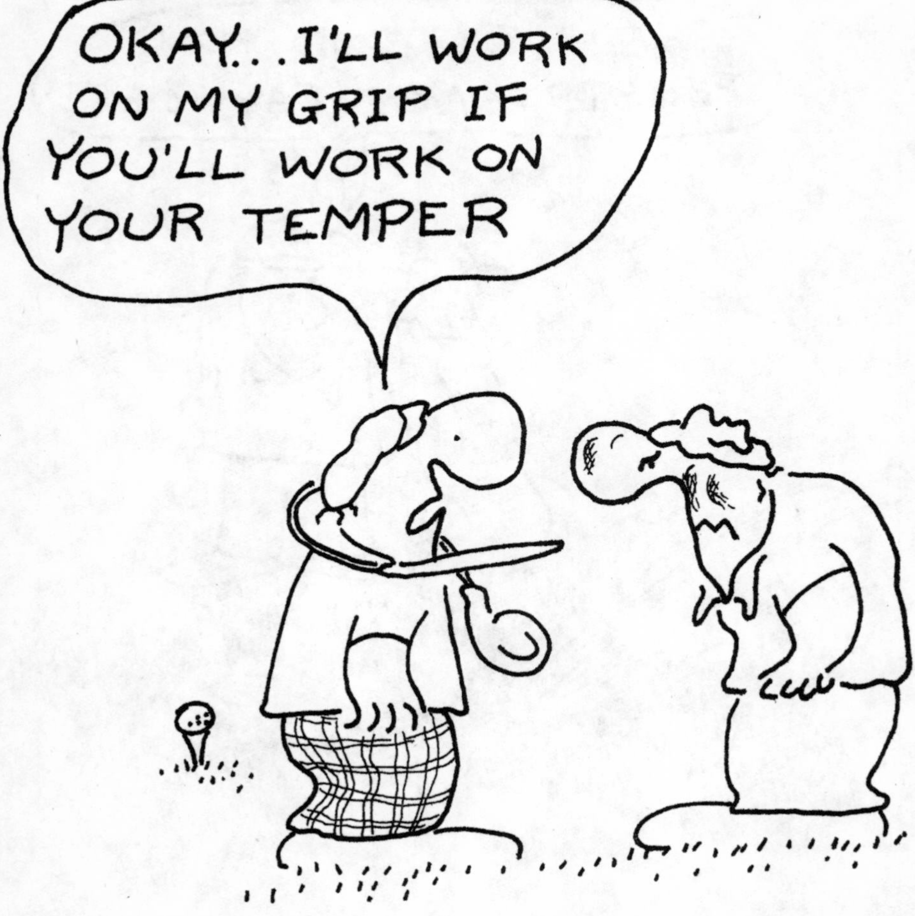
OKAY...I'LL WORK ON MY GRIP IF YOU'LL WORK ON YOUR TEMPER

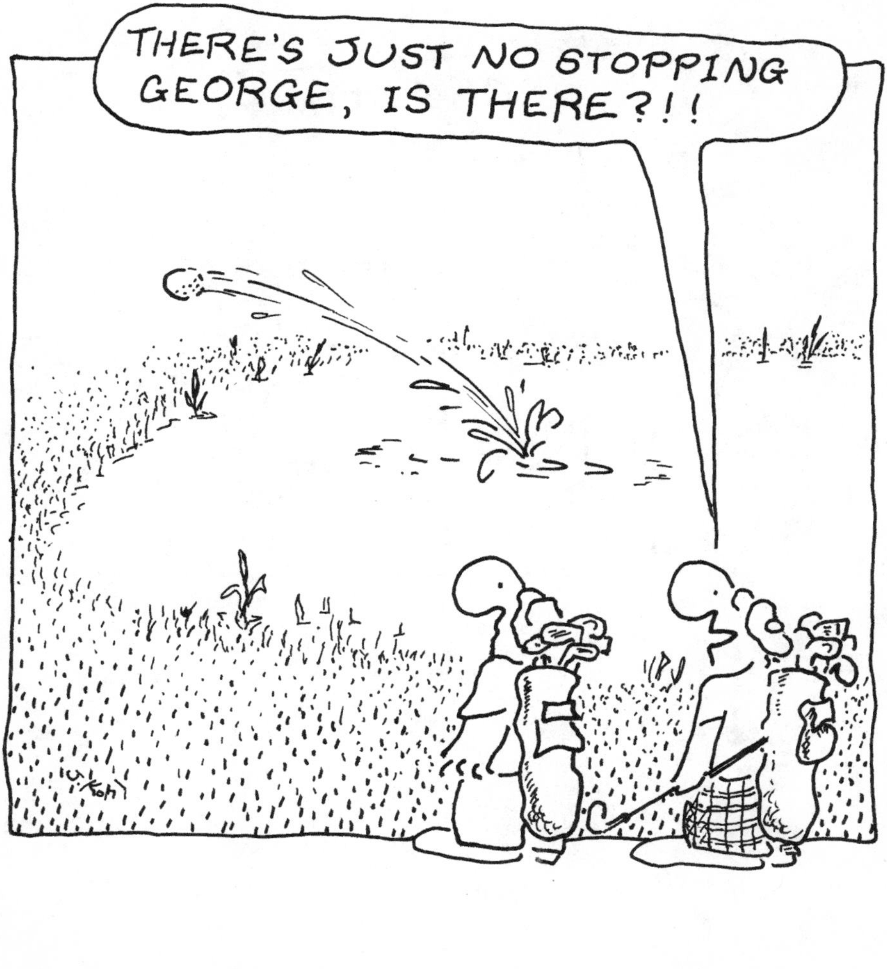
THERE'S JUST NO STOPPING GEORGE, IS THERE?!!

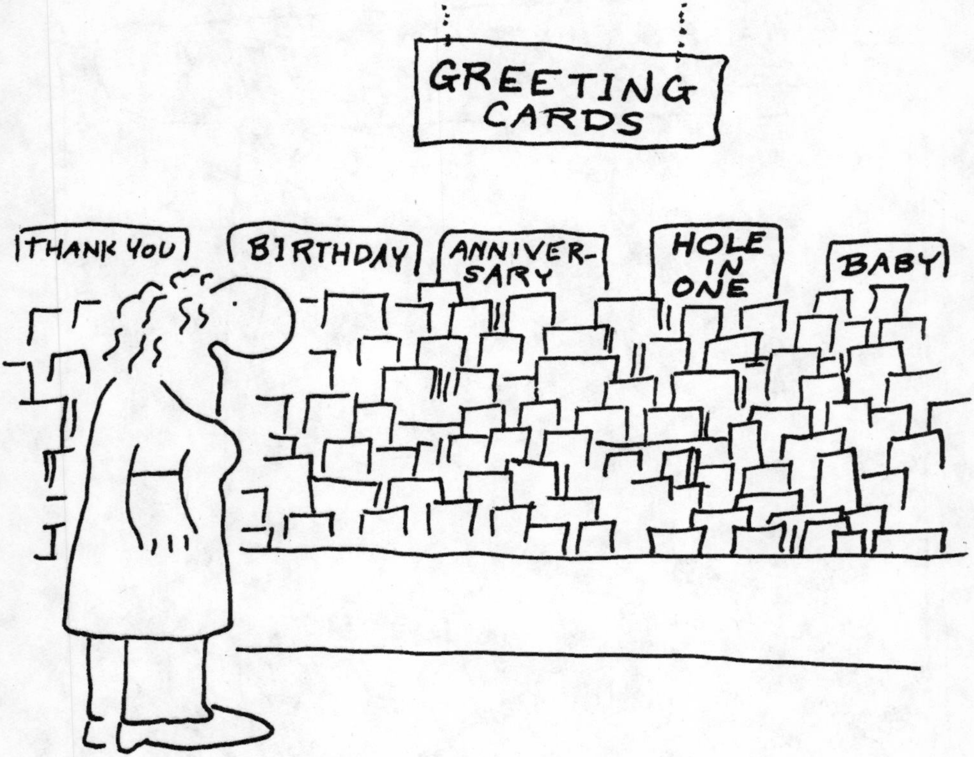
GREETING CARDS
THANK YOU
BIRTHDAY
ANNIVER-SARY
HOLE IN ONE
BABY

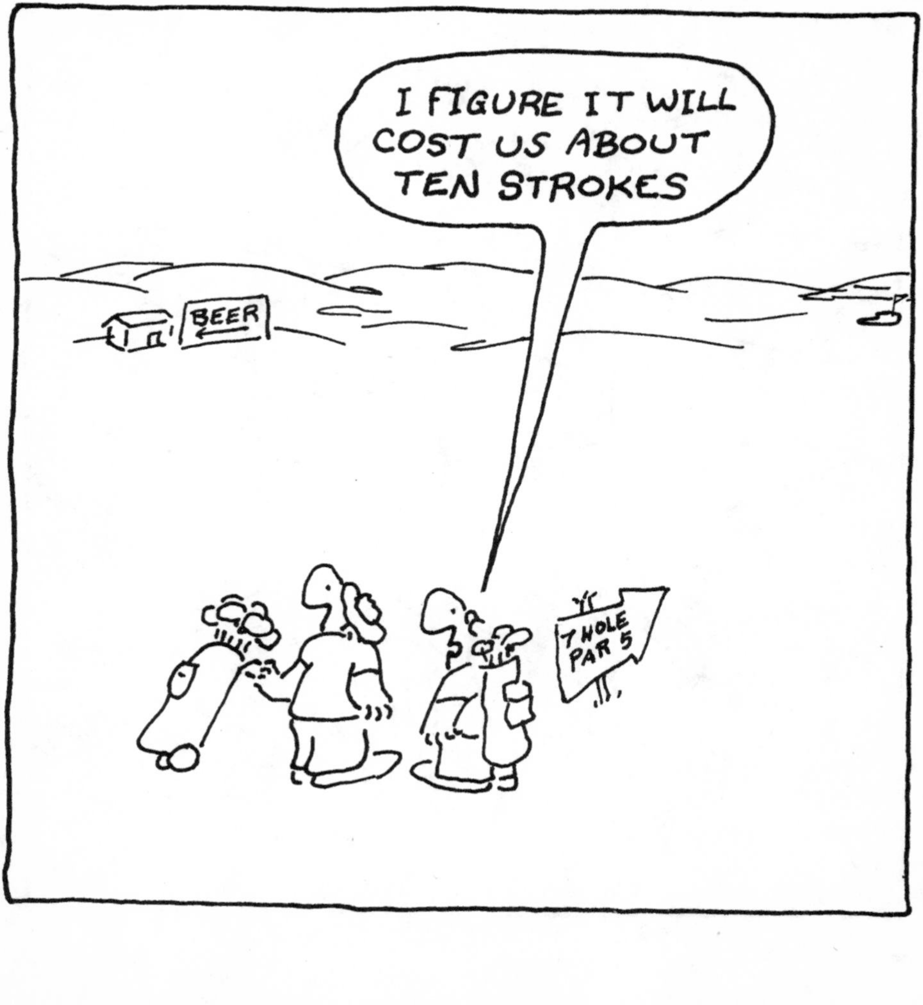
I FIGURE IT WILL COST US ABOUT TEN STROKES
BEER
7 HOLE PAR 5

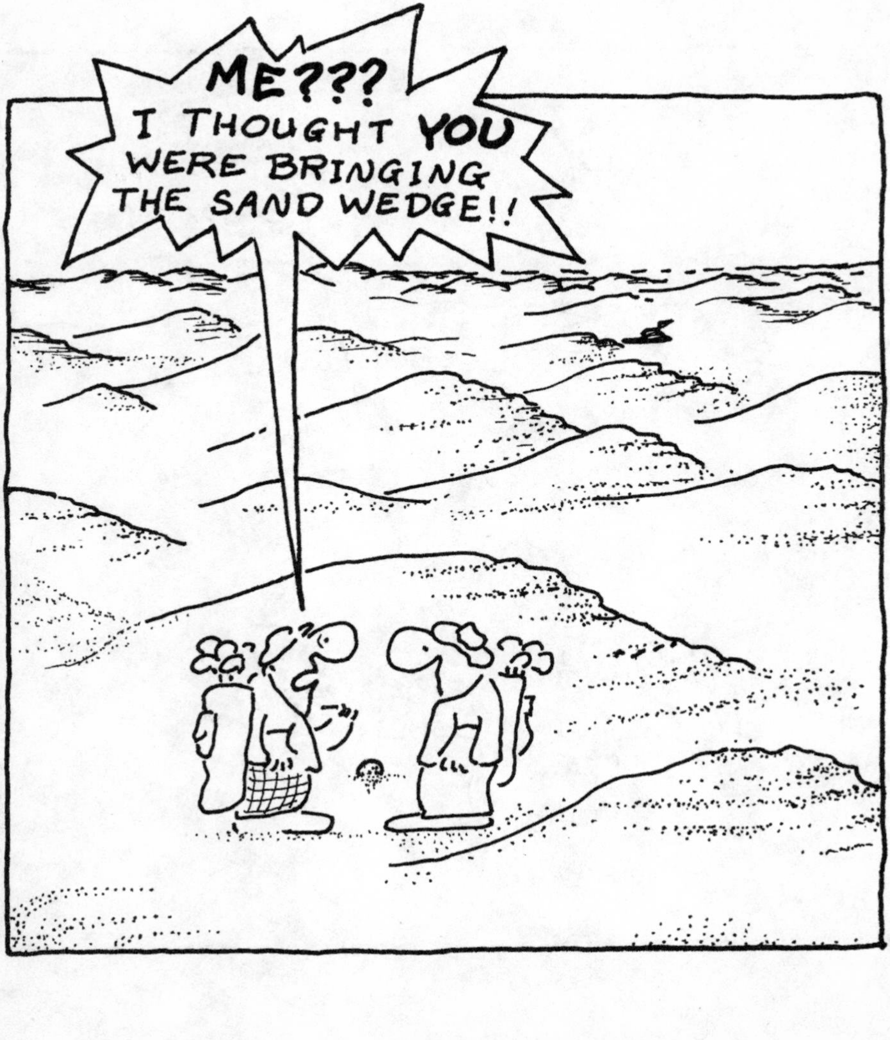
ME??? I THOUGHT YOU WERE BRINGING THE SAND WEDGE!!

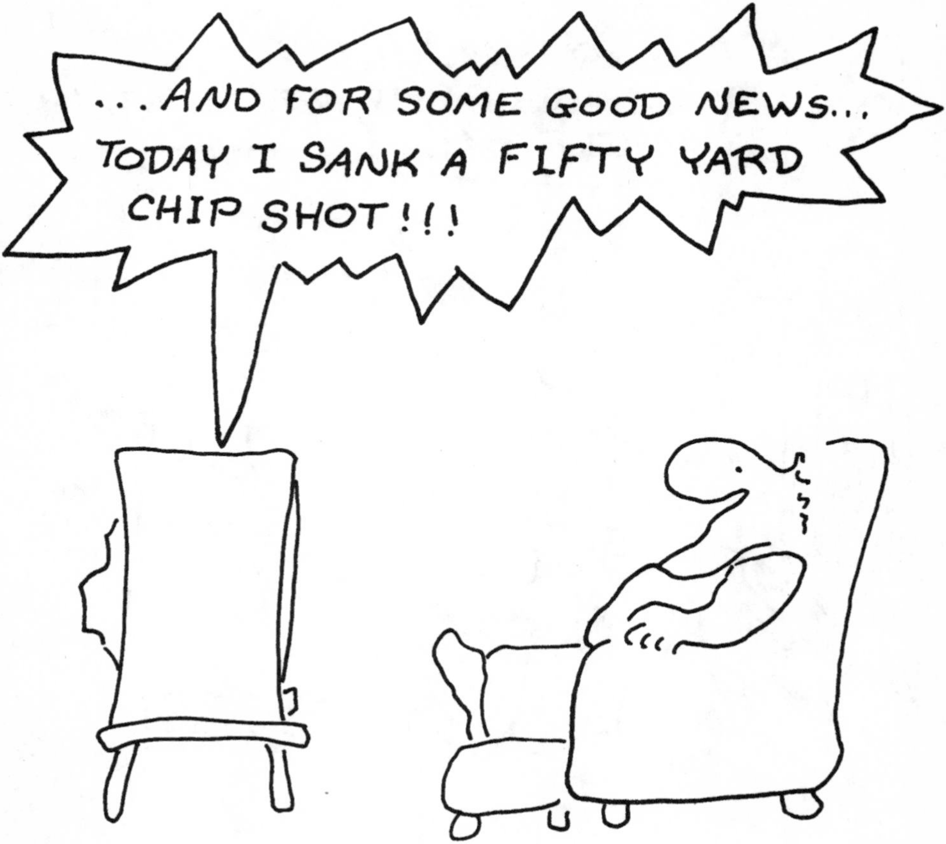
...AND FOR SOME GOOD NEWS... TODAY I SANK A FIFTY YARD CHIP SHOT!!!

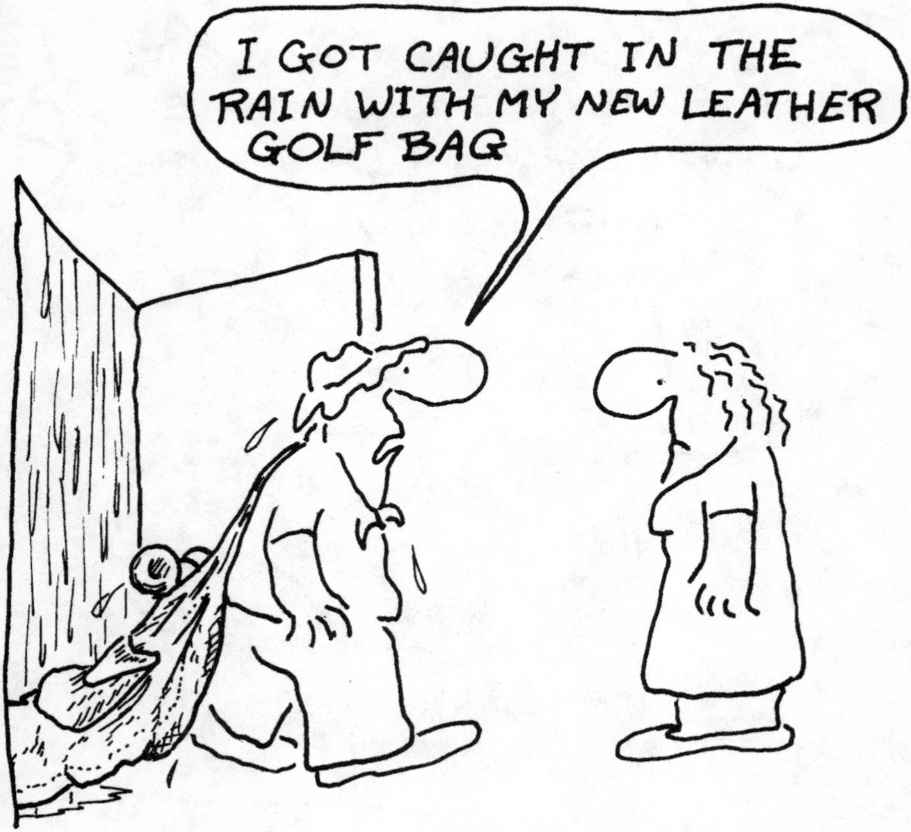
I GOT CAUGHT IN THE RAIN WITH MY NEW LEATHER GOLF BAG

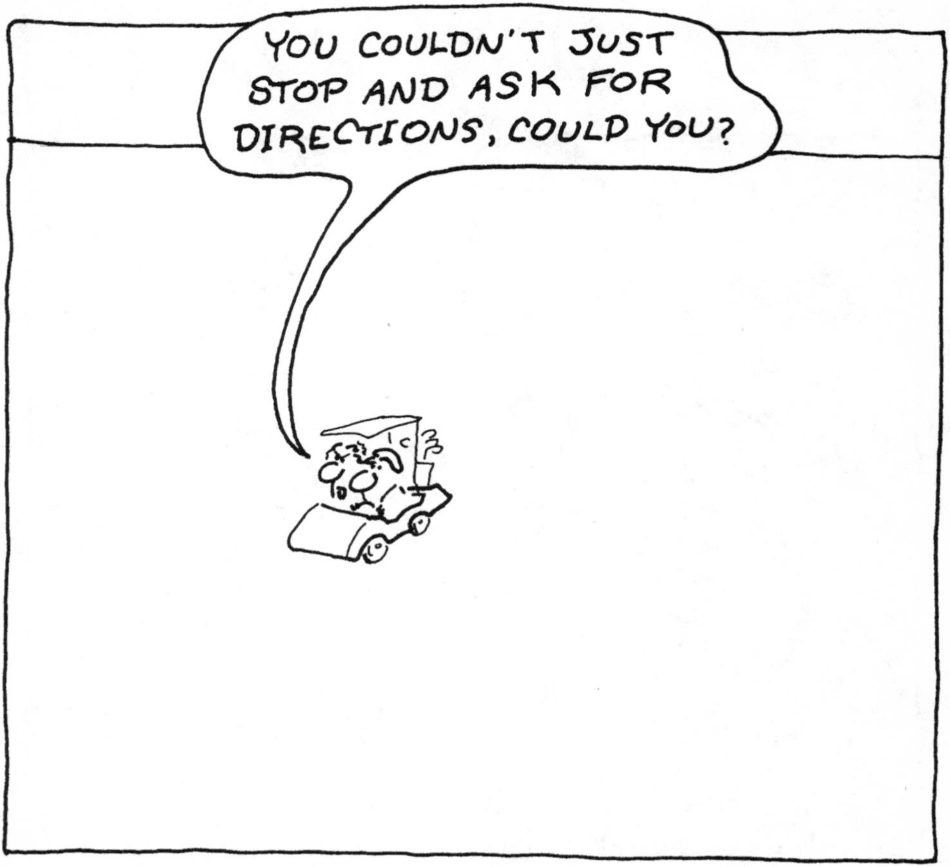
YOU COULDN'T JUST STOP AND ASK FOR DIRECTIONS, COULD YOU?

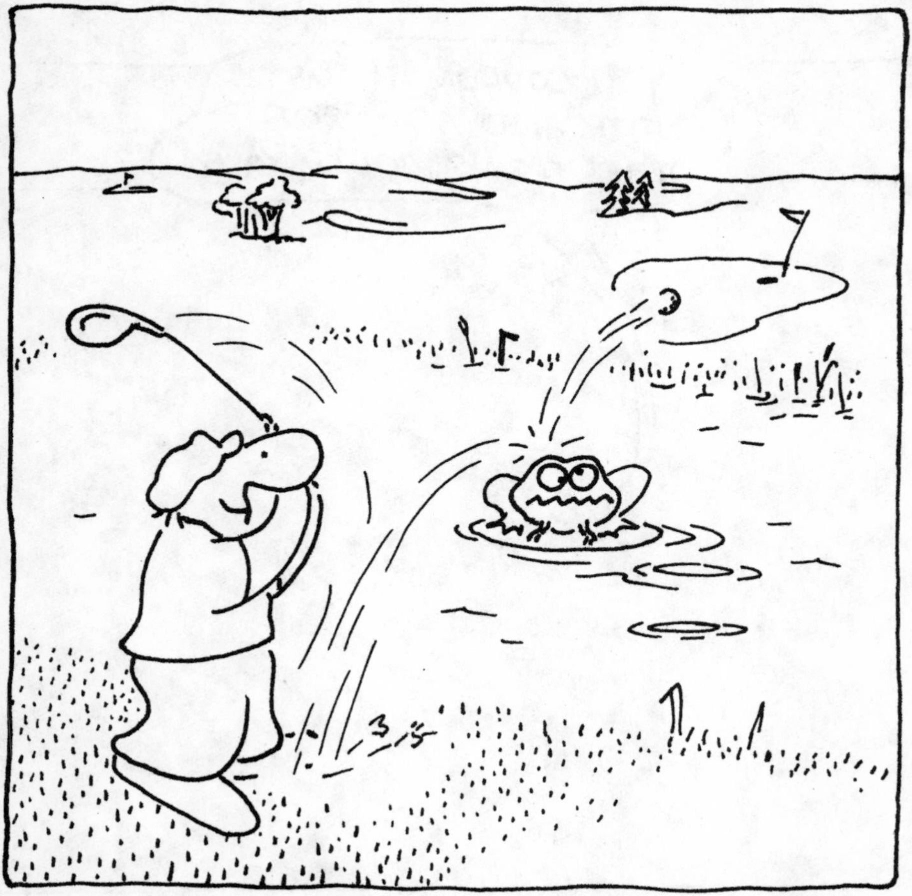

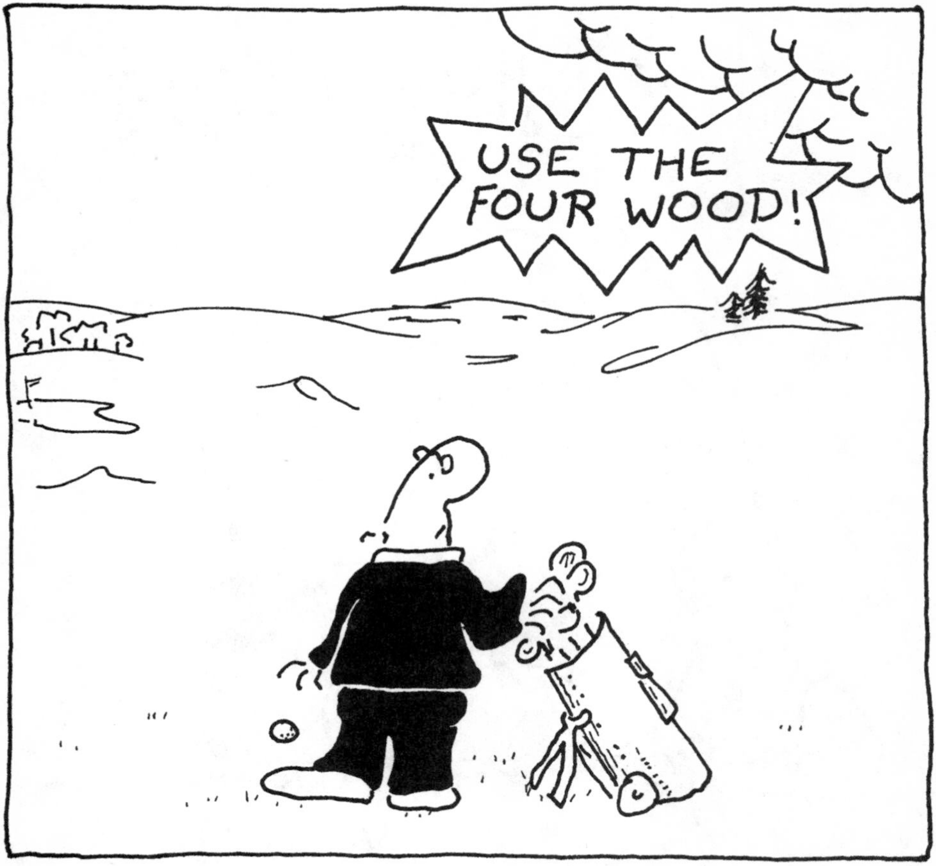
USE THE FOUR WOOD!

THE HUSTLER

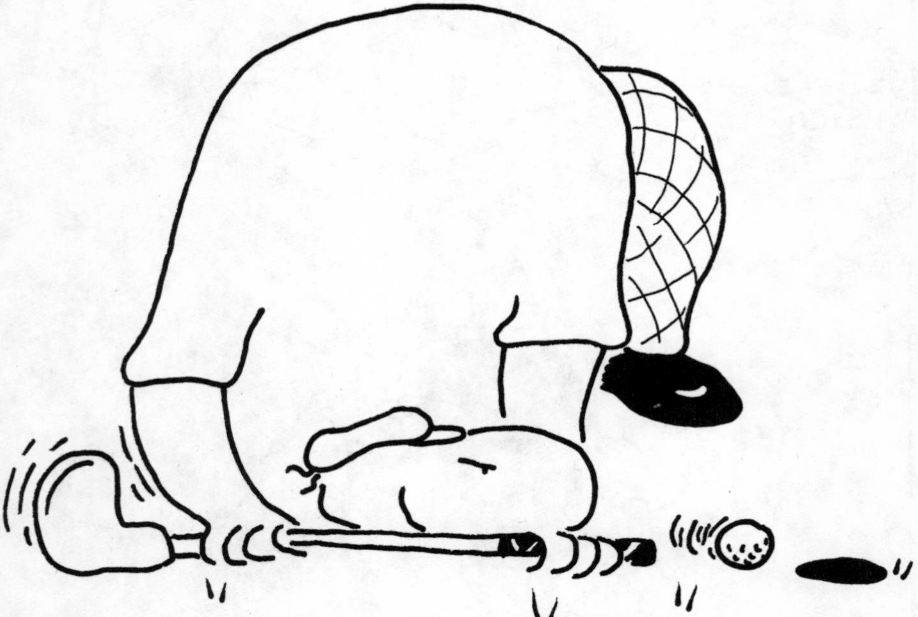

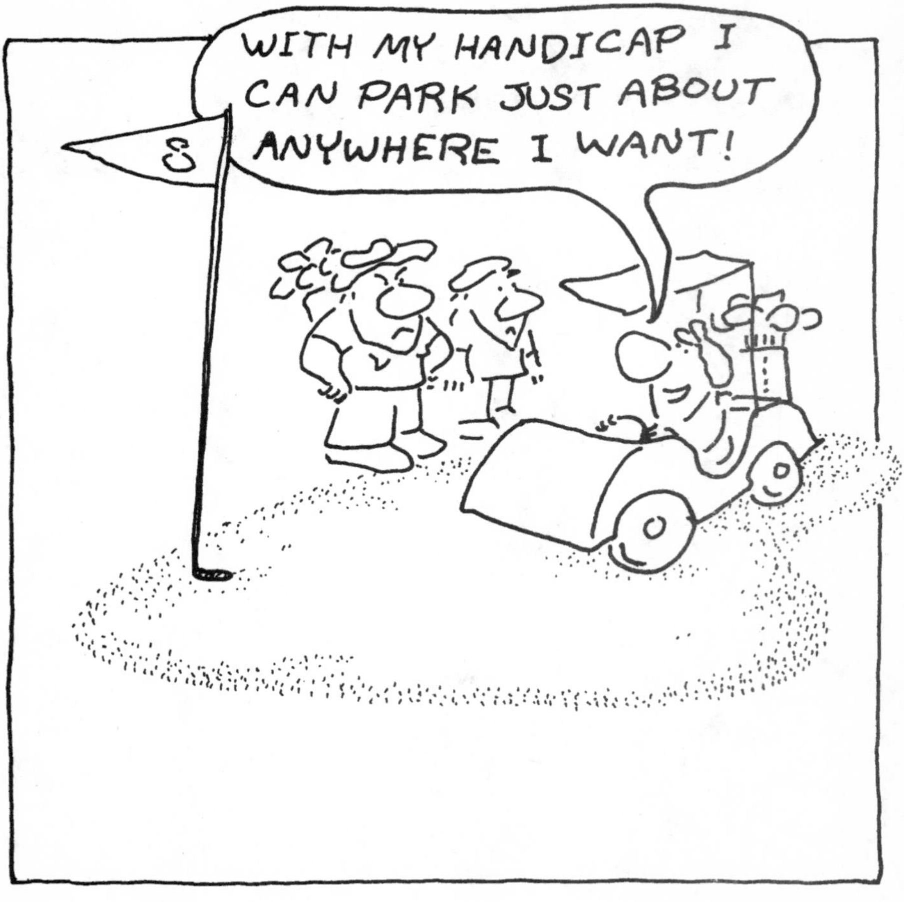
WITH MY HANDICAP I CAN PARK JUST ABOUT ANYWHERE I WANT!

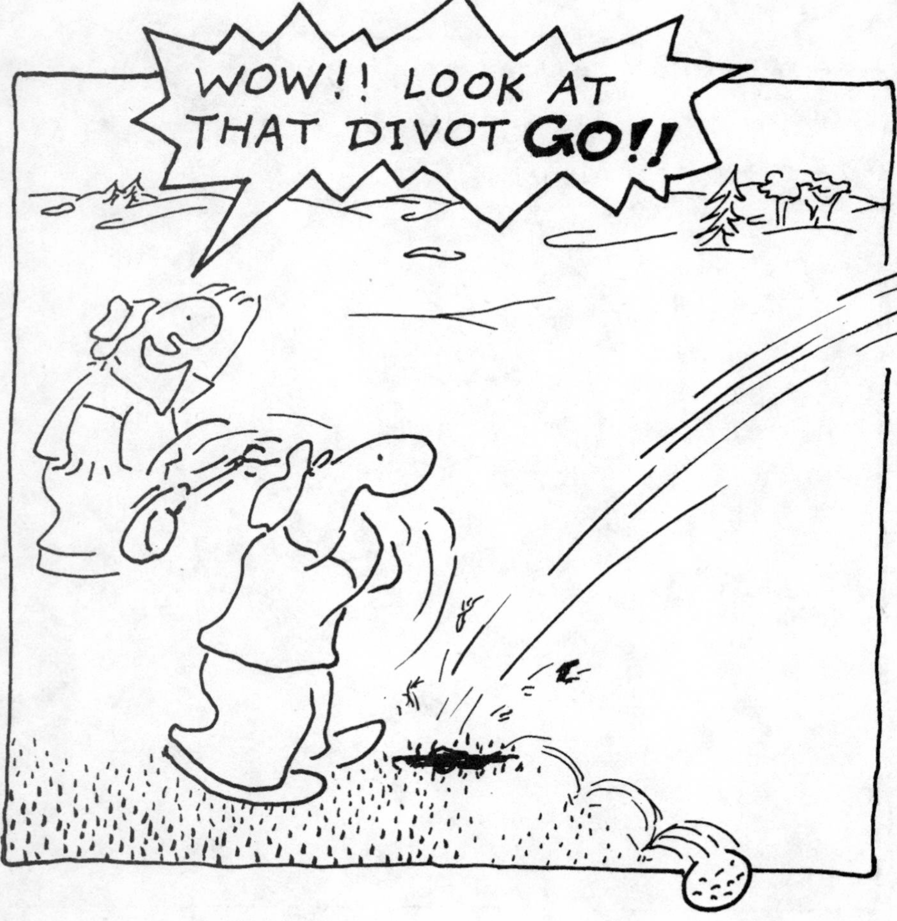
WOW!! LOOK AT THAT DIVOT GO!!

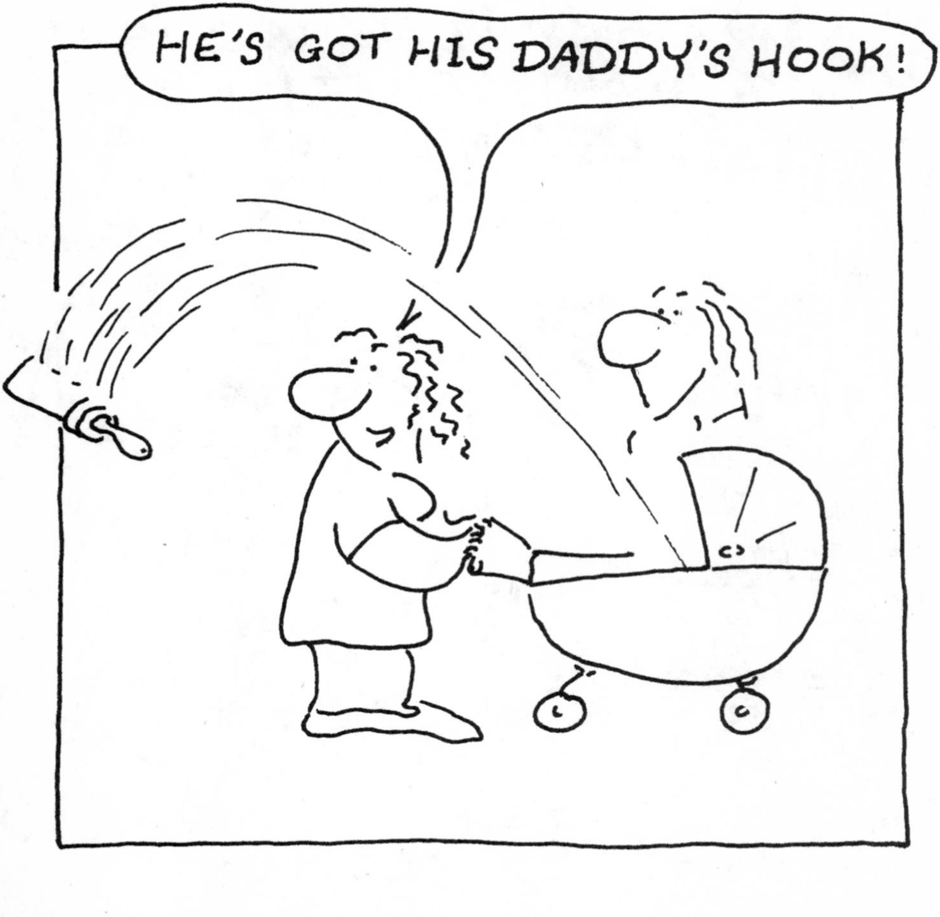
HE'S GOT HIS DADDY'S HOOK!

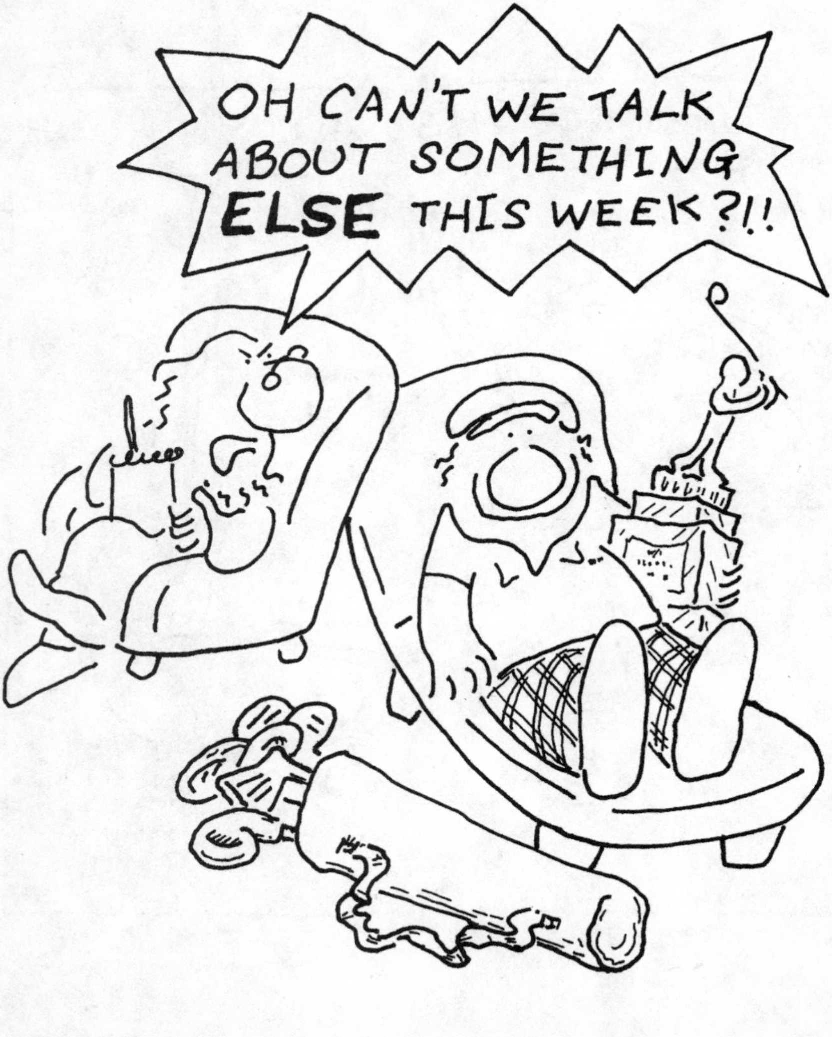
OH CAN'T WE TALK ABOUT SOMETHING **ELSE** THIS WEEK?!!

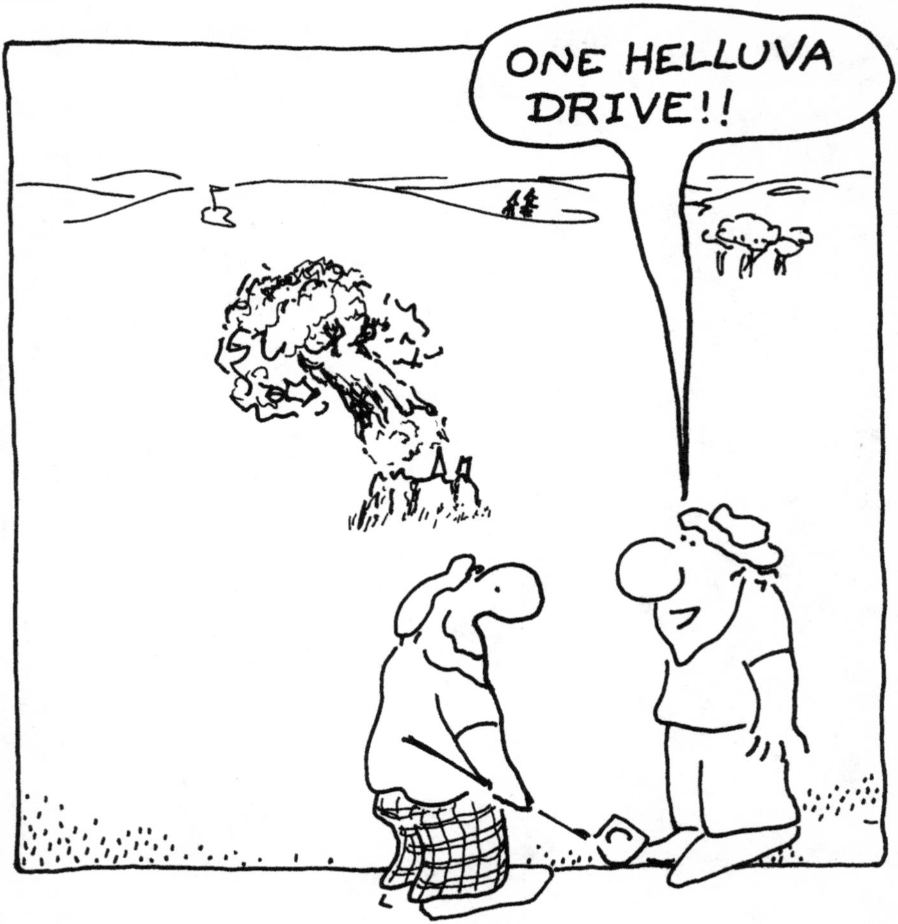
ONE HELLUVA DRIVE!!

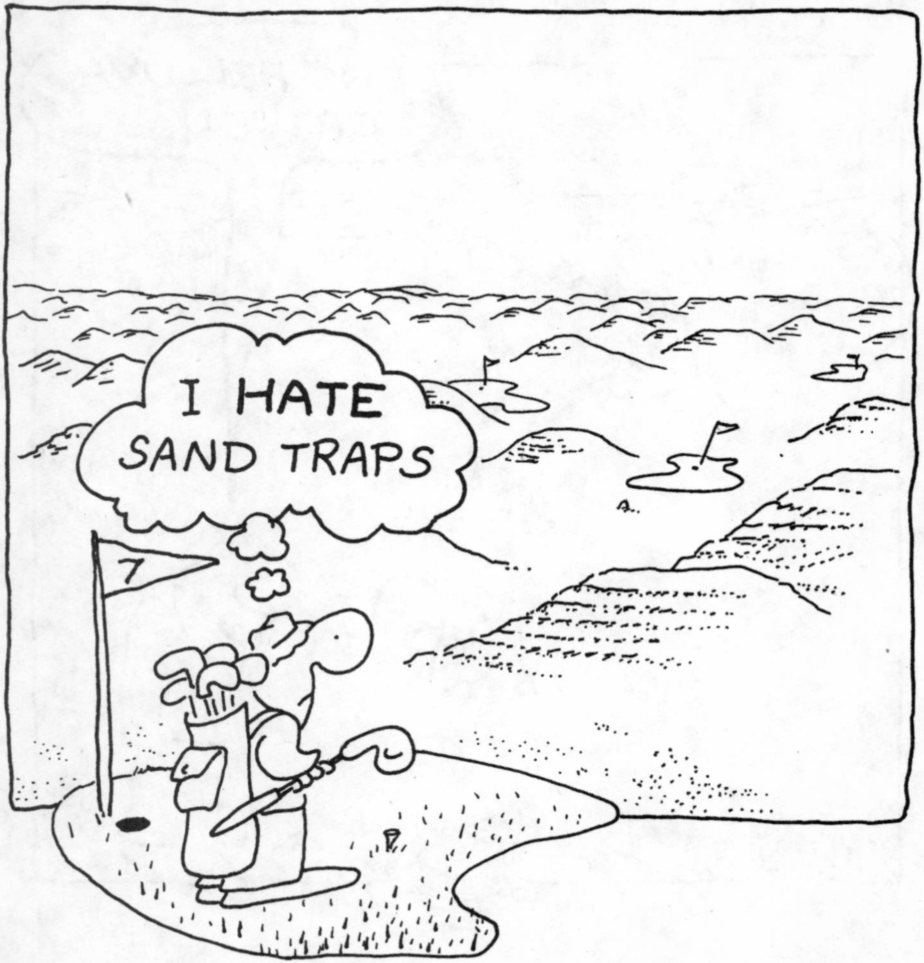
I HATE SAND TRAPS
7

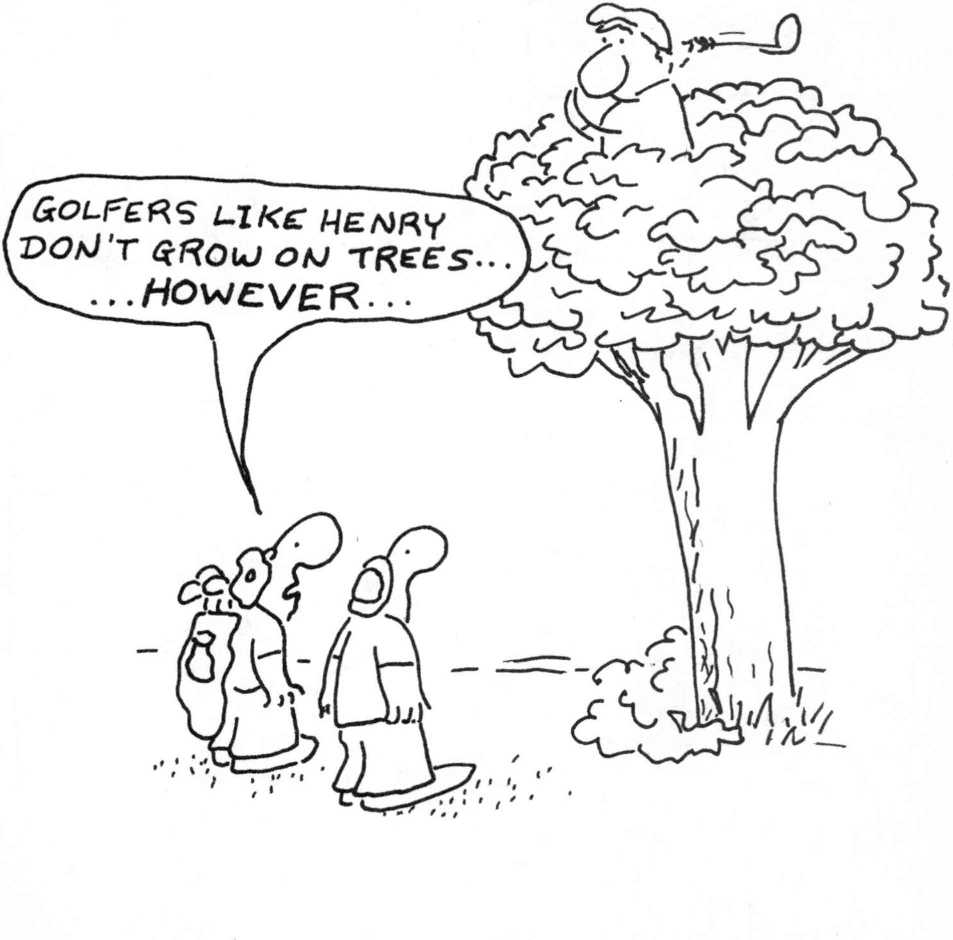
GOLFERS LIKE HENRY DON'T GROW ON TREES... ...HOWEVER...

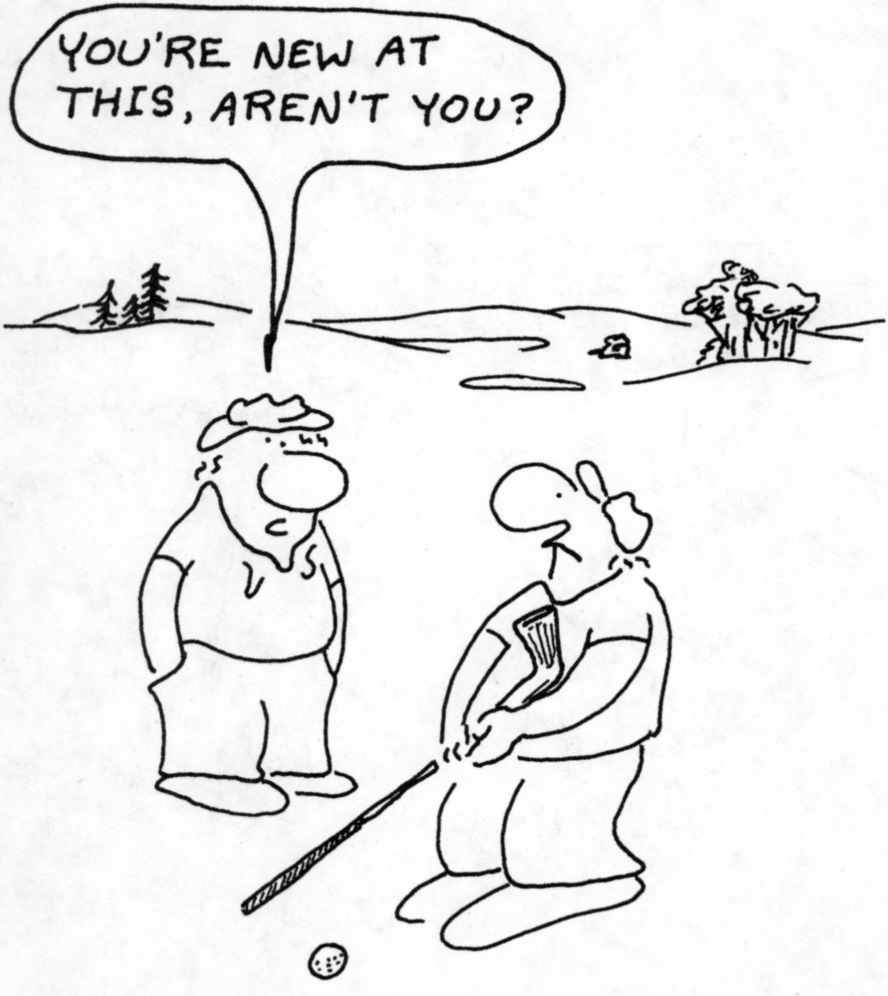
YOU'RE NEW AT THIS, AREN'T YOU?

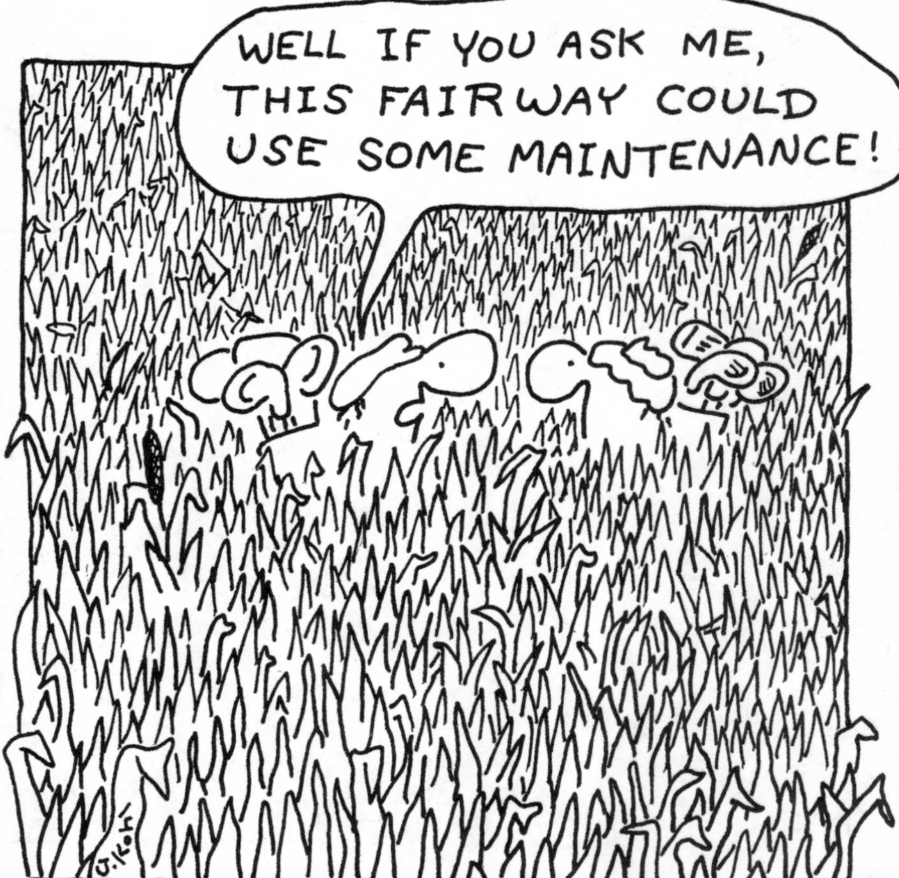
WELL IF YOU ASK ME, THIS FAIRWAY COULD USE SOME MAINTENANCE!
J. Koch

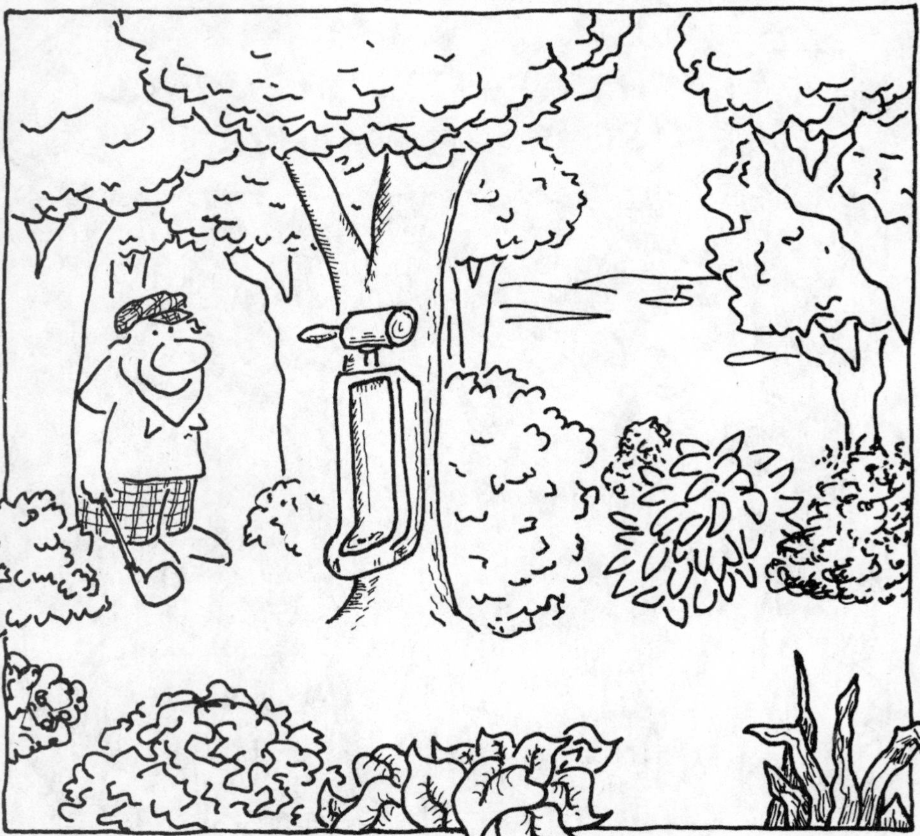

GOLF MYTH #473

THE PERFECT GAME

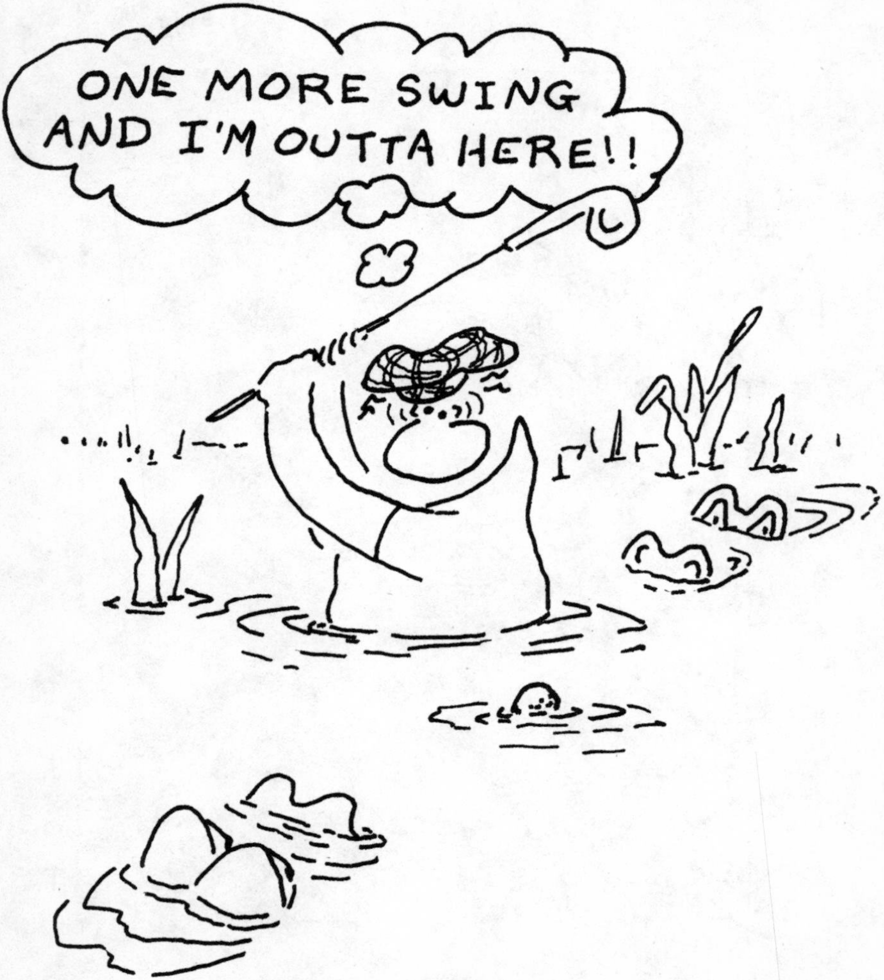
ONE MORE SWING
AND I'M OUTTA HERE!!

IT'S ONLY A GAME
IT'S ONLY A GAME
IT'S ONLY A GAME

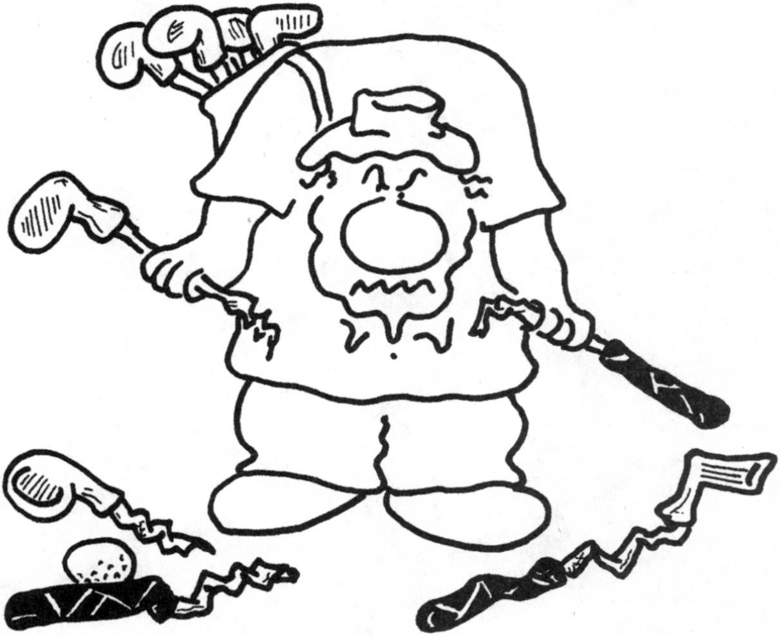

"One hundred years of experience
has demonstrated that
the game is temporary insanity
practiced in a pasture."
Dave Kindred

More Great Books
from Mustang Publishing

The Complete Book of Golf Games by Scott Johnston. Want to spice up your next round of 18 holes? With over 80 great betting games, side wagers, and tournament formats, this book will delight both weekend hackers and the totally obsessed. From descriptions of favorites like Skins and Nassau to details on unusual contests like String and Bingo Bango Bongo, it's essential equipment in every golfer's bag.
"A must acquisition."—Petersen's Golfing. **$9.95**

How to Be a Way Cool Grandfather by Verne Steen. There are some things a grandfather just <u>ought</u> to know: how to make slingshot from an old limb and a rubber band, how to make a kite from a newspaper, how to do a few simple magic tricks, and how to make his grandkids say, "Cool, Grandpa!" With complete details on making 30 fun, inexpensive toys, plus hints on using them to impart valuable lessons to kids, this is a great book for every old fogey who'd rather be way cool.
"A fun read...wonderfully presented."—Tucson Citizen. **$12.95**

The Complete Book of Beer Drinking Games by Griscom, Rand, & Johnston. With over 500,000 copies sold, this book reigns as the imbiber's bible! From classic beer games like Quarters and Blow Pong to wild new creations like Slush Fund and Beer Hunter—plus numerous funny essays and lists—this book is a party essential!
"The 'Animal House' of literature!"—Dallas Morning News. **$8.95**

Dear Elvis: Graffiti from Graceland by Daniel Wright. Writing a message to Elvis Presley on the wall of Graceland has become a tourist ritual, the American equivalent of kissing the Blarney Stone or throwing a coin in the Fountain of Trevi. From the hilarious to the heartfelt, these tributes to the King of Rock 'n Roll are must-reading for all fans—and anyone fascinated by the continuing phenomenon of Elvis Presley.

"We predict Wright's book is going to be one of those long-running best sellers...It's priceless!"—Elvis World. **$8.95**

Europe for Free by Brian Butler. If you travel on a budget — or if you just love a bargain — this book is for you! With thousands of things to do and see for free all over Europe, you'll save lots of lira, francs, and pfennigs.

"Well-organized and packed with ideas."—Modern Maturity. **$9.95**

Also in this series:
London for Free ($8.95) • DC for Free ($8.95) • Paris for Free ($8.95) • Hawaii for Free ($8.95) • The Southwest for Free ($8.95)

Mustang books should be available in your local bookstore. If not, send a check or money order for the price of the book, plus $2.00 postage **per book**, to Mustang Publishing, P.O. Box 3004, Memphis, TN 38173 U.S.A. To order by credit card, call toll free 800-250-8713 (or 901-521-1406). Allow three weeks for delivery. For rush, one-week delivery, add $2.00 to the total. **International orders:** Please pay in U.S. funds, and add $5.00 to the total for Air Mail.

For a complete catalog of Mustang books, send $1.00 and a stamped, self-addressed, business-size envelope to Catalog Request, Mustang Publishing, P.O. Box 3004, Memphis, TN 38173 U.S.A.